MEXICAN CRAVING

BEN MILBOURNE

MEXICAN CRAVING

New Holland

BEN MILBOURNE

CONTENTS

Foreword

When I first met Ben on the set of MasterChef Australia, it was immediately apparent that his enthusiasm for Mexican cuisine was a force to be reckoned with. He said he 'loved me', on national television, and at the time we hadn't even met! I'm pretty sure he was talking about the food I was cooking at my restaurant Mamasita.

Since then, Ben and I have become good friends, and I have learned that he has not only enthusiasm, but a great passion for Mexico and its food. It's passion that drives people to find the best in everything and Ben has found it in Mexican food. That's why I was thrilled to hear he was writing a book about food that I love too.

The culinary delights in Mexico have many guises and varieties. Just like European or Asian, it can range from robust country fare to subtle haute cuisine. It can be simple, complex, fiery, mild, earthy, zingy and zesty, and so on. One thing is for certain, it's always delicious, as you will no doubt find out within the pages of this book.

I have many cookbooks, at home and at work. Some books have given me inspiration, fresh ideas, and at times, guidance. As I have come to understand, recipes are simply a record of a moment in time. They are notes of an experiment that consisted of ingredients, tools, temperatures, time and ideas. Recipes, however, cannot explain or describe that moment your intuition comes into play, the moment your own knowledge and experiences tell you how much habañero to put in, that gut feeling telling you the pork is a little fatty so a little extra lime juice would be better for this one.

Good cooking is done with the head, the heart, the hands, and at times, with a reliable cookbook at your side. It's about creating great experiences combining the recipe with your own senses and desires. My cookbooks are full of little amendments, Post-it notes, scribbles, and some have un-decipherable sentences that I have trouble trying to translate. Regardless, they have all got a little something added from me, my chefs or my family. And all those little somethings come together to help deliver that memory I have of the dish so I can recreate the taste and that experience each time. Good cooking is about fun and enjoyment, and learning about how creative you actually are.

I know I'll be adding this book to my collection and jotting down within the pages my memories of the outcomes, and the moments that inspired and guided, and ended up being something to remember.

I'd like to make a toast to the success of Ben's first Mexican cookbook, no doubt the first of many.

Saludos.

Jason Jones
Co-owner of Mamasita and B'Stilla

TACO DE PESCADO FRITO CON ENSALADA VERDE
(CRUMBED FISH TACO WITH GREEN GARDEN SALAD)

This recipe is one that I frequently cook at home. I never managed to put it on the menu at Mamasita, as I couldn't use our fryer for fish. The inspiration for this combination comes from having a fried fish taco in Puerto Escondido, Mexico and trying to recreate it at home for my mother, using her garden vegetables.

6 corn tortillas (or as many as you can eat, just adjust the rest of the ingredients to suit)

2 limes, cut into wedges, to serve

oil for frying

CRUMBED FISH

200 ml/7 fl oz milk

2 eggs

½ bunch coriander/cilantro

100 g/3½ oz breadcrumbs (I use panko crumbs, Japanese breadcrumbs, but any will do)

salt to taste

120 g/4 oz plain/all-purpose flour, seasoned with a little salt and white pepper

200 g/7 oz white-fleshed fish, cleaned and cut into goujons (8 cm/3 in long thin strips)

SALAD

½ iceberg lettuce, washed and shredded

200 g/7 oz cucumber, cut into thin strips

1 green capsicum/bell pepper, cut into thin strips

2 avocados, flesh and seed removed, then sliced thinly

lemon juice

MAYONNAISE

4 egg yolks

30 ml/1 fl oz lime juice

zest of 1 orange

10 g/½ oz Dijon mustard

500 ml/17½ fl oz vegetable oil

salt and pepper

pinch cayenne pepper

chipotle seasoning (optional)

Recipe continued...

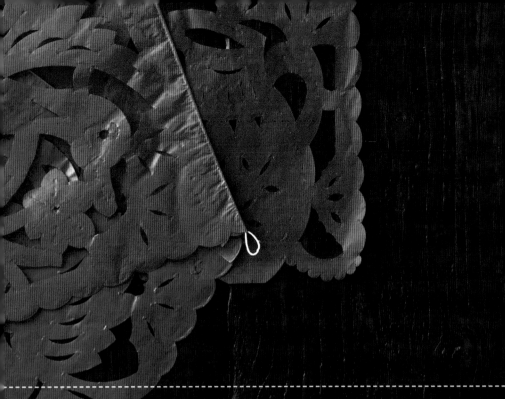

Whisk the milk and eggs together in a shallow bowl and set aside.

Wash and chop the coriander. Mix it into the breadcrumbs with a little salt.

Set up a crumbing station. Place the flour on a plate or shallow bowl, next to that the egg mixture, then the crumb/herb mix.

Toss each piece of fish in the flour, dip in the egg, then coat well with the crumbs. Set aside until ready to start frying.

Mix all the salad ingredients together with a little squeeze of lemon to prevent the avocado from discolouring. Set aside.

To make the mayonnaise, mix the egg yolk, lime juice, orange zest and Dijon mustard into a blender, turn on slowly.

Pour in the vegetable oil slowly to emulsify, then season with salt, pepper and cayenne (I like to add a little chipotle for mine).

Heat two pans. Put oil in one, about 1 cm deep, for frying the fish. The other is for the tortillas. When the oil is hot, carefully lay the crumbed goujons in the oil. Fry until golden. Remove and place on absorbent paper to remove excess oil. Heat tortillas in the hot, dry pan, about 30 seconds each side until the tortillas are hot, soft and flexible.

Dress the salad with just enough mayonnaise to coat the vegetables. Keep the remaining mayonnaise in the fridge for next time.

Place the heated tortillas on a board or on the bench. Place a little salad in each, then a couple of strips of fish. Fold and serve with a lime wedge on top. Sprinkle with extra cayenne.

Introduction

Mexican food came to me in a very odd way. My mother used to cook packet tacos, which was about as exotic as it got in my family, growing up on the North West coast of Tasmania in the 1990's. I loved them. We would only eat them during summer so there was this connection with school holidays and the fun that always comes with summer days and good times playing backyard cricket, swimming at the beach and fishing off the jetty. So as my culinary interests and skills developed as I got older, I started to venture away from the packet and started to experiment with more varied flavors and ingredients and discovered there is a lot more to Mexican cuisine than packet tacos, but from humble beginnings good things come.

Mexican food is all the rage at the moment and it's no wonder when you realise that Mexican food culture introduced the world to chocolate, corn, chillies, tomatoes, tomatillos, vanilla, avocado and guava. I am just scratching the surface of Mexican food—it is one of the oldest cuisines, yet it is one of the newest trends. It is the perfect food for sharing, which I think is one of the reasons I like it so much. It's packed full of flavour, it's healthy and it makes great use of seafood and slow braises—yet another reason I am so into it.

This book is a great introduction to Mexican-inspired food. It is not totally authentic, but it is my take on Mexican flavours designed to introduce you to the amazing world of Mexican cuisine in an achievable way. Some of the recipes require some authentic Mexican ingredients like chipotle and other dried chillies, tomatillos and masa harina. These ingredients are starting to become a little more common but if you can't find them you can purchase them online. I've also provided a list of substitutions (on the following page) so that if you don't have the authentic Mexican ingredients on hand, you can still create the Mexican flavours.

Substitute list

Replace this

Replace this	With this
1 teaspoon chipotle seasoning/chipotle powder	1 teaspoon smoked paprika and ½ teaspoon cayenne pepper
1 tablespoon achiote powder	1 teaspoon paprika, 1 teaspoon garlic powder, 1 teaspoon lime juice, ½ teaspoon salt, ½ teaspoon onion powder
queso fresco	ricotta
1 cup masa harina (for tostadas)	½ cup plain/all-purpose flour, ¼ cup fine polenta or semolina and ¼ cup corn flour
tostadas	round corn chips
1 whole ancho chilli	1 dried red chilli and 1 prune (just replace the chilli with these ingredients)
1 whole guajilla chilli	1 tablespoon sweet paprika
1 whole pasilla chilli	1 tablespoon paprika and 1 date (just replace the chilli with these ingredients)

My 8 Commandments

- Season to taste, or taste to season. Taste your food as you are cooking. Recipes are just a guide, but your palate should be your true inspiration. Taste your food as you cook and ask yourself does it need salt, sweetness, sour or spice and, most importantly, does it taste good.

- Start with the best key ingredients you can and don't stuff it up. Whichever ingredient is the key ingredient in the recipe try to get the best quality you can, talk to your supplier about the produce, what you are going to use it for and ask if they have any tips for preparing it.

- Cook because you enjoy it. Food is both a need and a want, we have to eat everyday so make it a celebration.

- Texture is taste. We say variety is the spice of life, so changing the texture of a dish helps to add that variety. Don't let your mouth get bored.

- You eat with all of your senses so it stands to reason that you should cook with them, touch, smell, taste, listen and look at your food as you cook it. This will give you a better understanding of what is happening at all stages of the recipe.

- Roasting and toasting is an essential part of Mexican cooking. Think of roasting and toasting the way you think of sautéing in French and Italian cooking. Roasting intensifies the flavour while toasting awakens the flavours that can be lost a little when things have been dried.

- You are what you eat, literally. Our body breaks down the food we eat to build the cells that make us so treat your body well, give it what it needs to build the best 'you' it can.

- Cook with someone. Cooking is a social thing and the process of preparing the food is actually the best time to be social. Sharing a coffee, a wine or a beer in the kitchen while preparing lunch, dinner or a snack—it's the best way to catch up.

MODERN TRADITIONS

Modern Traditions

Whenever I think of Mexican food the first things that come to mind are the three T's—tacos, tostadas and tortas. They are traditional street food and have been around forever but, as with most traditional foods, they lend themselves so well to modern interpretations.

The tacos that you may be most familiar with are the hard-shell corn variety, made infamous by packet dinners. These tex-mex creations aren't true tacos. True Mexican tacos are soft corn tortillas that are filled with anything your imagination can conjure, then folded in half to make that taco shape we all know and love. Small tacos are called taquitos and are perfect for canapés.

Tostadas are edible plates made from corn tortillas that are fried to make a flat disk, like a large corn chip. Toppings are then placed on the tostada and once you have eaten most of your meal you can munch on your 'plate' and there is no washing up to contend with. Small versions of tostadas are called tostaditas and are perfect for finger food or snacks.

Tortas are the Mexican version of a slider, small multi-layered burgers that incorporate different textures and flavours. Tortas are another way of putting your favourite ingredients in your hand so they're easy to eat.

Mostly they are made with masa harina, flour made from finely ground maize. There is also blue corn available which, when made into blue corn flour, gives your tortillas a blue-ish tinge.

HOMEMADE CORN TORTILLAS

250 g/9 oz yellow or corn masa harina
1 tablespoon salt flakes
500 ml/17½ fl oz warm water

Combine all the ingredients in a large bowl and mix with a wooden spoon or your hands to form a firm dough. Turn out the dough onto a floured surface and knead well for 5 minutes until it is no longer tacky. Place back in the bowl and cover with plastic wrap and allow to rest for 1 hour.

Pinch off portions of dough about the size of a golf ball. Roll them so they are reasonably symmetrical. If you have a tortilla press, open it and line it with silicon paper or baking paper/parchment and place the ball of dough in the middle and press down on the tortilla press.

If you don't have a press, place the ball of dough on a piece of silicon or baking paper/parchment and press down on it with your palm then place another piece of paper on top and roll out with a rolling pin until the tortilla is very thin.

Heat a large, dry frying pan over a medium heat and fry the tortillas as you make them. After 2 minutes, flip the tortilla—it should have a little colour. Fry the other side for 1 to 2 minutes. Place a clean tea towel on a plate and stack the tortillas there as you cook them, then wrap them in the cloth to keep them warm and stop them drying out.

Serve immediately or store in an airtight container, for up to 3 days. Reheat them again in a hot pan for a few seconds before use.

HOMEMADE FLOUR TORTILLAS

250 ml/9 fl oz milk

3 tablespoons olive oil

375 g/13 oz plain/all-purpose flour

2 teaspoons baking powder

2 teaspoons salt flakes

Combine the milk and oil in a small saucepan and warm slightly.

Combine all the dry ingredients in a large bowl, then pour the milk into the bowl and mix with a wooden spoon or your hands to form a firm dough. Turn out the dough onto a floured surface and knead well for 3 minutes until it is firm and no longer tacky. Place back in the bowl and cover with plastic wrap and allow to rest for 15 minutes.

Pinch off portions of dough about the size of a golf ball, roll them so they are reasonably symmetrical. If you have a tortilla press, open it and line it with silicon paper or baking paper/parchment. Place the ball of dough in the middle and press down on the tortilla press.

If you don't have a press, place the ball of dough on a piece of baking paper/parchment and press down on it with your palm then place another piece of paper on top and roll out with a rolling pin until the tortilla is very thin, about 2 mm or thinner.

Heat a large frying pan over a medium heat and fry the tortillas as you make them in the dry pan. After 2 minutes flip the tortilla—it should have a little colour. Fry the other side for 1 to 2 minutes. Place a clean tea towel on a plate as you dry-fry the tortillas and wrap them in the tea towel to keep them warm and stop them drying out as you go.

MAKES ABOUT 60

HOMEMADE TOSTADAS

I quantity Homemade Corn Tortillas
   (see recipe page 22)
oil, for frying
salt to season

To make tostadas, make tortillas following either the recipe for Homemade Corn Tortillas or Homemade Flour Tortillas. Cut the dry-fried tortillas into 5 cm/2 in rounds.

In a large, deep frying pan, heat oil until it is medium-hot and deep-fry in batches for 1 to 2 minutes. Drain on some paper towel and season with salt.

The tostadas will store in a cool dry place in an airtight container for up to a week.

The smaller deep-fried tostadas are sometimes referred to as tostaditas. Use these in any of the tostada recipes, or enjoy them on their own with your favourite salsa. You can also deep-fry a whole tortilla and use it as a tostada as well.

SERVES 4-6

POPCORN SHRIMP TACOS

oil, for frying

1 cup enoki mushrooms

24 fresh green prawns/shrimp, cleaned and
cut into 2 cm/1 in pieces

12 homemade corn tortillas

½ iceberg lettuce, shredded

Avocado Puree

1 tablespoon crème fraîche

1 teaspoon ground coriander seeds

2 ripe avocados

1 lime, juiced

1 tablespoon palm sugar

1 teaspoon salt

Corn and Mango Salsa

1 tablespoon butter

1½ cups corn kernels

1 mango, diced

1 cup coriander leaves

Batter

1 cup plain/all-purpose flour plus extra for
dusting

½ cup cornflour/cornstarch

1 tablespoon each of salt and
cracked black pepper

3 cups cold soda water or sparkling water

10 ice cubes

Make avocado puree by placing the crème fraîche, ground coriander seeds, avocado flesh, lime juice, palm sugar, 1 teaspoon of salt in a small blender and blend for 1 minute or until smooth.

To make corn and mango salsa, melt the butter in a saucepan over a medium heat. Add the corn and sauté for 5 minutes. Take off the heat and allow to cool before stirring through the mango and coriander leaves.

In a small saucepan, heat the oil over a medium heat and fry the enoki mushrooms—be careful as the oil will bubble and rise—until golden brown. Place on absorbent paper and season with salt.

To make the batter, mix the plain flour with the cornflour and 1 tablespoon each of salt and cracked black pepper. Make a well in the middle of the flour mix and add the soda water and ice. Coat the prawns in flour then dip in the batter mixture. Fry for 30 to 45 seconds in hot oil, then allow to drain on absorbent paper and season with salt.

Assemble the taco by placing 1 tablespoon of avocado puree down the middle of each tortilla, adding some shredded iceberg lettuce, followed by the corn and mango salsa, the popcorn prawns and finally the enoki mushrooms.

HUITLACOCHE TACOS

15 g/½ oz butter

15 ml/½ fl oz olive oil

150 g/5 oz Swiss brown mushrooms, sliced

2 corn cobs

1 large red chilli, deseeded and diced

1 x 400 g/14 oz huitlacoche (corn smut)

½ bunch coriander/cilantro, chopped

1½ cups Refried Beans (see recipe page 166)

12 Homemade Corn Tortillas (see recipe page 22)

1 teaspoon salt flakes

1 teaspoon cracked black pepper

1 cup grated sharp cheddar cheese

Heat the butter and oil in a large frying pan over a medium heat. Add the mushrooms and sauté for 5 to 10 minutes.

Cut the kernels off the corn by running a knife down the sides of the corn. Toss the corn, chilli and huitlacoche in with the mushrooms and sauté for another 5 minutes until cooked through. Turn off the heat and fold in the coriander.

To make the tacos, spread a spoonful of refried beans down the middle of each tortilla, spoon on the huitlacoche mixture, season with salt and pepper then sprinkle some cheese over the top and enjoy.

Huitlacoche is an essential ingredient in this, but if you don't have a tin on hand, you can add in some extra mushrooms, such as shiitake.

SERVES 4-6

GRILLED STEAK TACOS WITH CORN AND ROAST CAPSICUM SALSA

1.2 kg/2.6 lb skirt steak fillet
Garlic-lime-chilli Marinade (see recipe
    page 154)
olive oil, for frying
12 homemade corn tortillas (see recipe)
¾ cup yellow American mustard
½ bunch flat-leaf parsley, roughly chopped

CORN AND ROAST CAPSICUM SALSA
2 red capsicums/bell peppers
1 tablespoon olive oil
2 corn cobs
2 eschalots, diced
2 avocados, flesh and seed removed, flesh
    diced
juice of 2 limes
salt and pepper

Preheat the oven to 200°C/400°F.

Beat the steak with a meat mallet so it is a similar thickness all over, about 2 cm/5 in. Cover the steak with the garlic, lime and chilli marinade and leave it in the refrigerator for about 2 hours.

Brush the capsicums with some olive oil then place them on a lined oven tray and roast in the oven for 25 minutes or until they blister. Take them out of the oven and place in a bowl and cover with plastic wrap for 5 minutes then deseed and skin the capsicums and cut the flesh into strips (be careful as it will still be hot) and place in a bowl.

Heat a dry griddle pan to a medium heat and place a cob of corn in the pan. Allow to sit on one side for a minute until it starts to pop and slightly blacken then roll over and repeat on the other sides. Take out of the pan and cut the kernels off the cob. Repeat with the other cob of corn. Place all the corn kernels in a bowl with the capsicum and the eschalots, avocado, lime juice, olive oil and a little salt and pepper.

Take the steak out of the refrigerator and allow to get to room temperature. Heat a large frying pan to a high heat, drizzle the steak with some olive oil and place in the hot pan (make sure it sizzles). Leave it on one side for 2 minutes, then turn onto the other side for 3 minutes. Remove from the pan and allow to rest for 2 minutes under foil.

Once the steak has rested, cut it on the angle into 5 mm/¼ in slices. To serve, spoon some of the salsa onto the tortillas, then add 2 slices of the steak to each tortilla. Add a good drizzle of American mustard and a sprinkle of parsley.

CHICKEN SCHNITZEL TOSTADAS WITH AVOCADO PUREE AND CHORIZO CRUMBLE

6 chicken tenderloins

1 cup plain/all-purpose flour

2 eggs, lightly beaten

2 cups panko crumbs or breadcrumbs

oil, for frying

18 tostadas (or round corn chips, Mission are best)

1 cup shredded iceberg lettuce

¼ cup coriander/cilantro leaves

a pinch of salt flakes

AVOCADO PUREE

2 ripe avocados

juice of 1 lime

2 teaspoons palm sugar

salt and pepper

1 tablespoon crème fraîche

CHORIZO CRUMBLE

1 chorizo sausage, casing removed

Make the avocado puree by blending the flesh of the avocado in a blender with lime juice, palm sugar, salt and pepper to taste and then add the crème fraîche.

Make chorizo crumble by dicing the chorizo and placing it in a cold frying pan. Bring up the heat and fry the diced chorizo for 8 to 10 minutes until crispy. Allow to cool then blitz in a hand blender.

Use a meat mallet to gently tenderise the chicken and flatten it out. Cut each tenderloin in half. Place the flour, eggs and breadcrumbs in three separate shallow bowls. Coat the chicken pieces in the flour, then dredge it through the egg mix and finally coat in the breadcrumbs. Set aside on a plate until ready to fry.

Heat oil in a medium saucepan over a medium-high heat. Fry the chicken pieces for 2 minutes or until golden brown.

Assemble the tostadas by placing 1 teaspoon of avocado puree on top of each tostada, then a tablespoon of shredded lettuce, a piece of chicken schnitzel, another teaspoon of avocado puree, then the chorizo crumble and a coriander leaf. Sprinkle with a pinch of salt flakes before serving.

LAMB TOSTADAS WITH PERSIAN FETA, POMEGRANATE AND MINT

500 g/17½ oz lamb shoulder, cut into chunks

2 teaspoons salt flakes

1 teaspoon cracked black pepper

1 tablespoon olive oil

1 carrot, diced

1 brown onion, diced

3 cloves garlic, crushed

1 celery stick, diced

1 teaspoon ground coriander seeds

2 tablespoons tomato paste

2 cups vegetable stock

½ bunch thyme

3 bay leaves

8 tostadas (or round corn chips)

150 g/5 oz Persian feta

½ cup pomegranate seeds

½ cup toasted pepitas (pumpkin seeds)

¼ cup mint leaves

Season the lamb with the salt, pepper and olive oil. In a medium saucepan, brown the meat over a medium heat, remove and set aside.

In the same pan, sauté the carrot, onion, garlic and celery for 10 minutes on a medium heat until the onion is translucent. Put the lamb back in the pan and add the coriander and tomato paste and sauté for another 3 minutes. Cover with the stock, add the thyme and bay leaves and bring to a simmer. Place a lid on the pan and allow to lightly simmer for 2½ hours or until the lamb falls apart.

Take the lamb out of the saucepan and shred the meat using a fork. Set it aside. Heat a tablespoon of olive oil in a frying pan until it starts to shimmer. Fry the shredded lamb until it starts to caramelise and crisp up.

To serve, place a tablespoon of the fried lamb on top of a tostada then add some crumbled feta, pomegranate seeds, pepitas and finally a mint leaf.

TUNA TOSTADAS WITH CEVICHE SALSA AND PICKLED JALAPEÑOS

Ceviche Salsa
juice of 1 lemon
juice of 1 lime
2 coriander roots
1 clove garlic
2 cm/1 in piece ginger, peeled and chopped
1 green chilli
1 teaspoon salt
1 tablespoon palm sugar
1 Lebanese cucumber, deseeded and diced (reserve the seeds and juice)
2 eschalots, 1 diced
1 tomato, deseeded and diced
1 avocado, diced

Corn Puree
2 cups chicken stock
2 corn cobs, kernels removed
1 tablespoon cream

Pickled Jalapeños
½ cup white vinegar
½ cup caster/superfine sugar
2 jalapeños

150 g/5 oz fresh tuna, diced (the tuna is going to be slightly cured so you need to look for fish that has very little sinew)
1 tablespoon olive oil
salt and pepper
18 mini tostadas (5 cm/2 in diameter)
1 bunch coriander/cilantro cress (micro coriander)

- -

To make ceviche salsa, blend lemon juice, lime juice, coriander root, garlic, ginger, chilli, salt, palm sugar, the reserved cucumber seeds and juice and the whole eschalot in a food processor for a minute. It doesn't need to be smooth. Set aside for 15 minutes for the flavour to infuse then drain and collect the liquid. Mix 2 tablespoons of the liquid through the diced cucumber, tomato, diced eschalots and avocado.

To make the corn puree, bring the chicken stock to the boil and add the corn kernels. Simmer for 15 minutes, then drain and blitz in a food processor along with the cream then pass through a mesh sieve.

To make pickled jalapeños, bring the vinegar and sugar to the boil. Cut the jalapeños into thin slices and place in a heatproof bowl. Pour the sugar and vinegar mix over the jalapeños and allow to steep for 5 minutes, then drain.

To serve, combine the tuna, oil and 1 teaspoon each of salt and pepper. To each tostada add 2 teaspoons of corn puree, 2 teaspoons of the tuna mix and top that with 2 teaspoons of salsa and 1 slice of pickled jalapeño. Add some coriander cress to garnish.

MAKES 12

GORDITAS

1¾ cups masa harina
1½ cups warm water
2 tablespoons vegetable shortening
1 teaspoon salt flakes
1 teaspoon baking powder
¼ cup plain/all-purpose flour
oil for frying

Combine the masa harina with the warm water mix with a wooden spoon or hands to form a firm dough. Turn out the dough onto a floured surface and knead well for 5 minutes until it's firm and no longer tacky. Place it back in the bowl and cover with plastic wrap. Allow to rest for 30 minutes.

Mix the vegetable shortening, salt, baking powder and flour, then combine this mixture with the masa harina mix (you may need to add a little water for the two to come together). Portion and roll the dough into 12 equal balls.

Heat a medium frying pan over a medium heat. If you have a tortilla press, open it and line it with silicon paper. Place the ball of dough in the middle and press down on the tortilla press. If you don't have a press, place the ball of dough on a piece of silicon paper and press down on it with your palm then place another piece of silicon paper on top and roll out with a rolling pin until the gordita is a 5mm thick disc. Fry the gordita as you make them in a dry frying pan. After 2 minutes flip the gordita—it should have a little color. Fry the other side for 1 to 2 minutes.

Pour the oil into a frying pan, to the depth of about 2 cm/1 in, and heat to 170°C/340°F. Fry the gorditas—they will puff up and separate. Turn them after 30 seconds and fry for another 30 seconds then place on some absorbent paper and allow to cool for a bit then, with a sharp knife, cut an opening in the gordita. To serve, stuff them with whatever filling you want—salad, salsas, meat or seafood.

Gorditas are thicker tostadas that puff when they are fried—similar to pita bread. This creates a pocket that can be split and filled with whatever filling you want.

PULLED PORK TORTA WITH APPLE AND DAIKON SLAW

PULLED PORK

2 chipotle chillies

2 ancho chillies

2 guajillo chillies

1 x 400 g/14 oz can tomatoes

salt flakes

600 g/21 oz pork shoulder, roughly cut

pepper

olive oil

2 cloves garlic, minced

2 eschalots, diced

2 teaspoons ground coriander seeds

2 teaspoons ground cumin seeds

50 ml/1¾ fl oz apple cider vinegar

500 ml/17½ fl oz chicken stock

3 teaspoons palm sugar

2 teaspoons dried oregano

juice of 1 orange

APPLE AND DAIKON SLAW

2 Royal Gala apples, julienned

1 daikon, julienned

2 tablespoons kewpie mayonnaise

juice of 1 lemon

1 teaspoon chipotle seasoning

12 slider buns (or small dinner rolls)

12 baby butter lettuce leaves

2 medium tomatoes, sliced

small skewers

Make braising stock by toasting all the chillies in a dry pan for a couple of minutes each side. Place them in a bowl and cover with water. Allow to soak for 30 minutes. Once the chillies have softened, place them in a blender with the tomatoes and a pinch of salt. Blitz to make a puree.

Season the pork with salt, pepper and olive oil. Brown the meat in a large frying pan over a high heat. Once the meat has been browned, set aside.

In the same pan, sauté the garlic and eschalots in a teaspoon of olive oil for 2 minutes. Add the coriander and cumin and sauté for 1 minute to release the flavours. Add the vinegar and stock. Then add the tomato and chilli mix. Return the pork to the pan, adding the palm sugar and oregano. Check for seasoning and allow to simmer, covered, on the stove top or in an oven preheated to 150°C/300°F for 2 hours. Take off the lid and simmer for another 30 minutes or until the pork pulls apart and the sauce has reduced. Just before serving, add the orange juice as this will give the sauce a bit of a lift. Remove the pork shoulder and shred the meat using two forks.

To make the apple and daikon slaw, mix all of the ingredients together.

To assemble the tortas, cut the slider buns in half and place 2 tablespoons of pulled pork on the bottom, then add some lettuce, tomato, slaw and bun top. Skewer the torta so it stays together.

CHIPOTLE MEATBALL TORTAS

MEATBALLS
250 g/9 oz pork mince
250 g/9 oz beef mince
½ cup breadcrumbs
¼ cup oregano leaves
½ bunch coriander/cilantro stems, finely
  chopped
1 eschalot, diced
1 egg yolk
zest of 1 lime
1 tablespoon salt
1 tablespoon ground coriander seeds
1 tablespoon ground cumin seeds

CHIPOTLE SAUCE
3 rashers of bacon, diced
5 cloves garlic, minced
5 eschalots, diced

1 tablespoon chipotle seasoning
2 tablespoons dried oregano
2 x 400 g/14 oz crushed tomatoes
1 cup chicken stock
salt and pepper

SLAW
1 cup grated sharp cheese
½ cup kewpie mayonnaise
1 large carrot, julienned
½ red cabbage, shredded
½ green cabbage, shredded
juice and zest of 1 lime

8 small slider buns (or small dinner rolls)
small skewers

Place all the ingredients for the meatballs in a large bowl and, using your hands, combine everything thoroughly. Roll into small meatballs and place on a plate or tray and put in the refrigerator until ready to use.

Place the bacon in a cold pan and bring up to a medium heat. Once some fat has rendered out add the garlic and eschalots and sauté for 5 minutes. Add the chipotle seasoning, oregano, tomatoes and the chicken stock and bring the sauce to a simmer. Add the meatballs and simmer for 10 minutes, or until the sauce thickens enough to hold everything together. Season with salt and pepper, to taste.

In a small bowl, make the slaw by combining cheese, mayonnaise, carrot, both types of cabbage and lime juice and zest. If the slaw is too wet add some more cabbage and carrot.

To assemble your tortas, slice the slider buns in half. On the bottom half place three meatballs, then add on some slaw. Add the top slider bun and hold everything in place with a small skewer.

This recipe may make more meatballs than you need. Serve the leftovers with red rice or smashed potatoes, or even spaghetti. Or store them in the refrigerator or freezer.

SERVES 4-6

BFC (BEN'S FRIED CHICKEN) TORTA

1 cup plain/all-purpose flour

1 tablespoon salt flakes

1 tablespoon cracked black pepper

1 tablespoon ground coriander seeds

1 tablespoon ground cumin seeds

1 tablespoon chipotle seasoning

1 tablespoon dried thyme

6 chicken thigh fillets, deboned

½ cup milk

12 slider buns (or small dinner rolls)

6 strips streaky bacon, cut in half

oil, for frying

salt, to season

½ cup kewpie mayonnaise

12 baby butter lettuce leaves

2 medium tomatoes, sliced

1 small red onion, cut into rings

oil, for frying

12 small skewers

Combine the flour, salt, pepper, ground coriander and cumin seeds, chipotle seasoning and dried thyme in a shallow medium bowl.

Beat the chicken thighs with a meat mallet so they are about ½ to 1 cm thick. Cut them in half. Pour the milk into a bowl, dip in the chicken pieces and then coat them in the flour mix.

Cut the buns in half and toast them cut-side down in a dry frying pan over medium heat, this will help keep the buns dry and give them a nice crunch.

Fry the streaky bacon until it crisps up then set aside.

Heat the oil to 170°C/340°F. If you don't have a thermometer, drop a pinch of flour in the oil, it should bubble straight away and turn brown within 5 seconds. Then deep-fry the flour-coated chicken in a large saucepan or deep fryer for 2 minutes or until golden brown. Place on some absorbent paper and season with salt.

Spread some mayonnaise on the bottom buns. Add a piece of fried chicken, a lettuce leaf, a tomato slice or two, onion rings and bacon strip. Place the top half of the bun on each bottom and skewer it to keep them together.

STREET FOOD
AND SNACKS

Street Food *Antojitos*

Mexican cuisine lends itself perfectly to street food or snack food. Food on the go is ingrained in the culture; you could even say that the cuisine is designed to be easy to eat. Antojitos, the name that is given to snack food, literally means 'on a whim', or 'a sudden craving'. In Mexico, antojitos are broken down into 8 specific food items, which all incorporate the hugely important ingredient corn masa or masa harina (corn dough). These foods are tacos, quesadillas, enchiladas, tostadas, sopes, gorditas, chilaquiles and tamales.

SERVES 4

ABALONE ALBONDIGAS

250 g/9 oz abalone, roughly chopped

1 egg yolk

3 cloves garlic, grated

2 cm/1 in knob of ginger, grated

½ bunch coriander/cilantro stalks, finely chopped

1 teaspoon ground anato seeds or achiote seasoning

1 teaspoon each salt and pepper

2 cups breadcrumbs plus extra for crumbing

1 cup plain/all-purpose flour

1 tablespoon each salt and pepper

2 eggs, beaten

2 L/4 pints of vegetable oil for frying

Place the abalone in a high-speed blender and blitz into a smooth paste.

Place the abalone paste, egg yolk, garlic, ginger, coriander, ground anato seeds, a teaspoon each of salt and pepper and breadcrumbs into a mixing bowl and mix together until well incorporated. You may need to add more breadcrumbs if the mixture is too wet to handle.

Roll the abalone mix into balls about the size of a tablespoon. In a shallow bowl, add a tablespoon each of salt and pepper to the flour. Roll the abalone balls in the flour, dip in the beaten egg and then roll them in some more breadcrumbs. Place on a plate ready for frying.

In a large saucepan, heat the oil to 170°C/340°F and fry the abalone balls for 1 minute or until golden brown. Season with salt as they come out of the pan and serve with lime or chipotle mayo (see Lime Mayonnaise recipe page 148).

SOPES

2 cups masa harina
1 tablespoon salt flakes
1¾ cups warm water
oil, for baking
your choice of fillings, salsas and sauces

Combine masa harina, salt and warm water in a large bowl and mix with a wooden spoon or hands to form a firm dough. Turn out the dough onto a floured surface and knead well for 5 minutes until the dough is firm and no longer tacky. Place back in the bowl and cover with plastic wrap and allow to rest for 1 hour

Pinch off portions of dough about the size of a golf ball, roll them so they are reasonably symmetrical. If you have a tortilla press, open it and line it with silicon paper. Place the ball of dough in the middle and press down on the tortilla press. If you don't have a press, place the ball of dough on a piece of silicon paper and press down on it with your palm then place another piece of silicon paper on top and roll out with a rolling pin until the tortilla is about 7 mm/¼ in or thinner.

Heat a large pan over a medium heat and fry the tortillas as you make them in a dry pan. After 30 seconds flip the tortilla—it should have a slight crust, fry the other side for 30 seconds then remove from the pan.

The tortillas will have a slight crust but the dough will still be raw, pinch the slightly raw dough around the edge of the tortilla to make a wall (similar to a pie crust) around the outside of the tortilla, creating a sope.

Return the sopes to the pan and cook for another 45 seconds then place on a baking tray, drizzle with oil and top with your favorite toppings. Bake in the oven for 8 to 10 minutes.

Sopes are similar to testadas but they are thicker and have an edge to hold the filling in, this means they are a little heartier and can hold a bigger array of toppings

BEANS ON TOAST

1 red capsicum/bell pepper
olive oil
1 chorizo, cut into rounds
2 eschalots, diced
2 cloves garlic, minced
1 red chilli, cut into rounds
1 x 400 g/14 oz can red kidney beans
1 x 400 g/14 oz can crushed tomatoes
4 sprigs thyme

1 tablespoon chopped parsley
salt and pepper
sourdough bread, to serve

Rub the capsicum with olive oil and roast in the oven at 180°C/350°F until the skin blisters. Take it out of the oven, place it in a bowl and cover with plastic wrap. Leave covered for 5 minutes. Then peel the skin off, remove the seeds and set aside.

Place the chorizo in a cold pan and bring the heat up to medium, as you do this some oil will leach out of the chorizo. Once you get heat into the pan add the eschalots, garlic and chilli, using the oil to gently fry for 5 minutes or until the onion softens.

Add the beans, tomatoes and thyme and bring to a simmer. Simmer for 5 minutes. Scatter through the parsley, season with salt and pepper and serve with some toasted sourdough.

SERVES 4-6

BEER BUBBLE OYSTERS

1 cup plain/all-purpose flour, plus extra for
   dusting
½ cup cornflour/cornstarch
2 teaspoons salt flakes
2 teaspoons black pepper

2 teaspoons ground coriander seeds
300 ml/10½ fl oz strong beer such as a pale ale
10 ice cubes
12 natural oysters, in shell

Combine the flours, salt, pepper, coriander, beer and ice and mix until smooth. The mixture should resemble thick paint.

Preheat the oil to 170°C/340°F. If you don't have a thermometer, test the oil is ready by dropping a pinch of flour into the oil, it should bubble straight away and turn brown within 5 seconds. Dust the oysters in flour and coat in the batter. Fry in oil for 1 minute then drain on absorbent towel and place back in the shell to serve.

You could serve this with some lime mayo (see Lime Mayonnaise recipe page 148).

CHIMICHANGAS

500 ml/17½ fl oz chicken stock or water

2 chicken breasts

2 chipotle chillies

1 tablespoon oil

2 onions, diced

4 cloves garlic, diced

1 teaspoon ground cumin

1 teaspoon ground coriander

½ teaspoon ground cinnamon

½ teaspoon ground cloves

1 teaspoon salt flakes

1 teaspoon cracked black pepper

1 x 400 g/14 oz can crushed tomatoes

1 x 400 g/14 oz can pinto beans

¼ cup queso fresco (ricotta)

8 Homemade Flour Tortillas (see recipe
  page 27)

¼ bunch coriander/cilantro, chopped

oil, for frying

Bring the chicken stock to the boil in a medium saucepan. Place the chicken and chipotle in the stock and bring back to the boil. Cover with a lid and turn the heat off and leave for 15 minutes. Take the chicken and chillies out of the liquid, shred the meat and chop the chillies. Set aside.

Heat the oil in large frying pan and fry the onions until translucent then add the garlic, spices, salt and pepper and cook for 3 minutes. Add the tomatoes and pinto beans and cook for 10 minutes. Add the chicken, chillies and queso fresco and check for seasoning.

Soften the tortillas in the microwave or a dry frying pan so they are pliable. Spoon some chicken mixture into the middle of a tortilla then fold the side facing you up, and then fold the sides in, like you are wrapping a present. Sprinkle with chopped coriander. Place it fold side down as you repeat with the rest of the mixture and the tortillas.

Heat some oil in a large frying pan then shallow-fry the parcels until they are golden and crunchy.

CORN AND CRAB QUESADILLAS WITH MANGO SALSA

CHIPOTLE SAUCE

2 cloves garlic, diced

oil, for frying

1 x 400 g/14 oz can crushed tomatoes

2 teaspoons chipotle seasoning

SALSA

3 Roma tomatoes, deseeded and diced

1 avocado, diced

juice of 1 lime

2 spring onions/scallions, diced

1 mango, diced

3 teaspoons palm sugar, grated

¼ cup coriander/cilantro leaves

QUESADILLA

200 g/7 oz crabmeat, fresh or thawed if using frozen

2 teaspoons corn kernels

1 red chilli, diced

2 cloves garlic, diced

zest of 2 limes

½ cup coriander/cilantro leaves, chopped

1 cup Manchego cheese, roughly grated

4 Homemade Flour Tortillas (see recipe page 27)

Preheat oven to 220°C/420°F.

Make the chipotle sauce by sautéing the garlic in a saucepan with a little oil then add the tomatoes and simmer for 2 minutes. Finally add the chipotle seasoning and set aside.

For the salsa, combine all the ingredients in a medium bowl and set aside.

Combine all the quesadilla ingredients, except the tortillas, in a bowl. Spread 2 tablespoons of chipotle sauce on 1 tortilla, cover with half of the crab mixture and place a second tortilla on top. Heat a large non-stick dry frying pan over a medium heat and carefully place the tortilla in it. Cook for 2 minutes each side then transfer to a lined baking tray and place in the oven for 3 to 5 minutes. Repeat with the rest of the filling ingredients and 2 remaining tortillas.

Once cooked, cut the quesadilla in half or thirds (so they are in triangles) and serve with salsa.

SERVES 6

CRUSTY CORN

6 corn cobs
225 g/8 oz butter
2 tablespoons olive oil
1 teaspoon salt flakes
1 teaspoon cracked black pepper
2 cloves garlic, crushed
1 cup multigrain breadcrumbs
¼ cup chopped coriander/cilantro leaves
½ cup finely grated parmesan

Place the corn in a large pan of salted boiling water until tender, about 12 minutes, then drain and allow to cool.

Melt the butter in a pan and add the olive oil, salt, pepper and garlic and stir. Pour the butter into a shallow dish.

Combine the breadcrumbs and coriander in a shallow bowl. Roll each corn cob in the butter so it is coated then roll them in the breadcrumbs. Finish the corn on a hot barbecue or griddle pan for about 5 minutes, turning regularly, until the crumbs are golden. Or place in the oven at 200°C/400°F for 8 minutes, until the breadcrumbs are golden. Serve with grated parmesan over the top.

SERVES 6

EMPANADAS

Dough
1 cup masa harina
2 tablespoons plain/all-purpose flour
1 teaspoon salt
35 ml/1 fl oz oil
150 ml/5 fl oz warm water

Filling
1 tablespoon oil plus extra for deep-frying
½ onion, finely diced
2 cloves garlic, minced
250 g/9 oz pork mince
2 ancho chillies, chopped
1 teaspoon ground cumin seeds
1 teaspoon ground coriander seeds
1 teaspoon salt flakes
3 tomatoes, deseeded and diced

Mix together the masa harina, flour, salt, oil and the warm water to make a dough. Knead for 5 minutes then set aside to rest for 30 minutes.

To make the filling, heat a tablespoon of oil in a medium pan. Add the onion and garlic and sauté for 3 minutes then add the mince, chillies, cumin, coriander and salt. Cook for another 2 minutes then add the tomatoes and cook for a further 5 minutes. Remove from the heat and set aside.

Roll the dough into small balls about the size of a small golf ball, then flatten out into rounds, about 7 to 8 cm/2¾ to 3 in wide, with a tortilla press or a rolling pin, about ½ cm/¼ in thin. Place a spoonful of the filling in the middle of the round, brush the edge of the rounds with water then fold the round in half and press down and pinch around the edges to seal.

To fry the empanadas, heat up some oil in a medium pan until very hot. Deep-fry the empanadas in batches until crispy.

SERVES 6

POPPERS

6 fresh poblano chillies, jalapeño chillies or
    small capsicums/bell peppers
2 potatoes, peeled and diced into
    1 cm/¼ in cubes
200 g/7 oz cream cheese
200 g/7 oz sharp cheese
1 tablespoon sweet paprika
1 bunch chives, finely chopped
1 teaspoon each salt and pepper

2 eggs, separated
1 cup plain/all-purpose flour
oil, for frying

Make a neat cut in the chillies or capsicums and place them in a hot pan, turning until the skins blister, then place them in a bowl and cover with plastic wrap for 10 minutes. Carefully scrap the seeds out through the cut in the side and peel the skins off the chillies and set them aside.

Place the potatoes in a medium pan of cold water and bring to the boil. Cook the potatoes until just tender then drain thoroughly.

Mix the cream cheese, cheddar cheese, sweet paprika and the chives together with a teaspoon of salt and a teaspoon of pepper. Add the potatoes and gently combine. Spoon the mixture into the chillies via the cut in the side until full and the chilli fits comfortably around the cheese mixture. Place in the refrigerator for an hour.

When ready to cook, whisk the egg whites until stiff peaks form. In a separate bowl, whisk the egg yolks until pale then fold them into the egg white to make the frying batter.

Heat the oil to 180°C/350°F. If you don't have a thermometer, test to see if the oil is ready by dropping some batter into the oil—it should bubble as soon as it hits the oil.

Dust the chillies in flour then cover in the batter and fry in oil, until golden brown.

Serve with an ice-cold beer.

SERVES 4

MOLETTES

4 finger rolls/dinner rolls
50 g/1¾ oz butter
250 g/9 oz Refried Beans (see recipe
  page 166)
1 cup grated sharp cheddar cheese

1 avocado, diced
juice of 1 lime
pinch of salt and pepper

SALSA
1 tomato, deseeded and diced
1 small white onion, diced
¼ cup coriander/cilantro leaves,
  finely chopped

Cut the rolls through the middle and open them up, spread them with butter. Heat a medium pan and fry the rolls, butter-side down, for 2 to 3 minutes or until dark brown and crusty.

In a small saucepan, heat the refried beans until warmed through over a medium heat. Spoon the beans onto the toasted roll, sprinkle with grated cheese and place under the grill for 1 to 2 minutes.

Make the salsa by combining all of the salsa ingredients in a bowl.

Take the molettes out from under the grill, spoon some salsa over the top and serve.

CHILAQUILES

1 tablespoon olive oil

1 brown onion, diced

1 clove garlic, diced

1 jalapeño pepper, deseeded and diced

1 x 400 g/14 oz crushed tomatoes

1 teaspoon dried oregano

1 stick cinnamon

1 cup water

salt, to taste

1 quantity Homemade Tostadas (see recipe page 28) or 100 g/3½ oz of good quality thick corn chips

1 white onion, diced

¼ cup chopped coriander

50 g/1¾ oz queso fresco

2 tablespoons crème fraîche

In a large pan, heat the olive oil over a medium heat then sauté the brown onion, garlic and jalapeño until the onion is translucent. Add in the tomatoes, oregano, cinnamon and water. Bring to a simmer for 5 minutes. Season with salt to taste.

Add the tostadas or corn chips to the pan and simmer for another 5 minutes so the tostadas or chips have some time to soak up the sauce but don't get soggy.

Place the tostadas and sauce mixture in a serving dish and garnish with the white onion, coriander, queso fresc and crème fraîche.

Chilaquiles are the closest thing you will find to nachos in Mexico

POTATO CAKES

600 g/21 oz all-purpose potatoes, skin on

1 cup grated cheddar cheese

1 teaspoon salt flakes

50 g/1¾ oz pickled jalapeños, chopped

1 egg, beaten

small bunch of fresh coriander/cilantro,
    finely chopped

flour, for dusting and shaping

oil, for shallow frying

salsa, to serve

Place the potatoes in a large saucepan of cold water. Bring the water to the boil and allow to simmer for 25 minutes or until tender. Drain the potatoes. When cool enough, peel them and cut them in half. Mash or pass them through a mouli ricer.

Stir the cheese into the potatoes along with the salt, jalapeños, egg and coriander.

When the mixture cools, roll tablespoons of the mixture into balls and flatten. Roll them in some flour, to coat, and flatten them a little. Heat some oil in a large frying pan and fry the potato cakes for about 2 minutes on each side.

Serve with a little salsa or mayonnaise (see Salsas, Sauces and Sides chapter) of your choice.

MEXICAN SCRAMBLED EGGS

8 eggs

3 cloves garlic, finely diced

1 cup crème fraîche

2 tablespoons olive oil

1 cup deseeded and diced tomatoes

½ white onion, finely diced

1 ripe avocado, deseeded cut into 5 mm
   diagonal slices

½ cup coriander/cilantro leaves, chopped

salt and pepper

sourdough bread, to serve

Whisk the eggs, garlic and crème fraîche until well combined.

Heat a large pan to medium, add half the olive oil and then add the egg mixture. Allow the egg to catch and soufflé then drag it into the middle of the pan, allowing more egg mixture to move on to the hot pan. Cook the eggs halfway (about 2 minutes) then fold in the tomatoes and onion.

Spoon the eggs onto the plate and add the avocado and coriander leaves, season and drizzle with the remaining extra olive oil.

Serve immediately with sourdough toast soldiers.

SERVES 4-6

PUMPKIN LATTE

1 onion, diced

2 cloves garlic, diced

1 teaspoon paprika

½ chilli

25 g/¾ oz butter

350 g/12 oz pumpkin, grated

2 cups chicken stock

1 cup cream, lightly whipped

salt and pepper

ground nutmeg, in a shaker

¼ cup coriander/cilantro leaves, chopped

Place the onion, garlic, paprika, chilli and butter in a saucepan and sweat on a low heat until the onion is soft and translucent. Add the pumpkin and cook for 2 to 5 minutes or until the pumpkin is soft and breaks apart between your fingers when you squeeze it.

Add the stock and bring to a simmer. Add the cream and blitz the soup with a hand blender or bar mix. Season with salt and pepper.

Pour the soup into a latte glass, dust with nutmeg and serve with a pinch of chopped coriander.

SERVES 6

CHILLI DOG

6 hot dog buns

6 hot dog frankfurters

2 chipotle-braised beef cheeks, with a little
   sauce (see Chipotle-Braised Beef Cheek
   with Oven-roasted Tomatoes and Smashed
   Potatoes recipe page 114)

1 cup grated sharp cheddar cheese

Cut the hot dog buns vertically down the middle and set aside. Cook the hot dogs according to packet instructions, you can either place them in boiling water, or on a griddle pan or frying pan.

Shred the beef cheek with 2 forks and fold it through some of the adobo sauce from the beef cheek recipe.

Place the frankfurters inside the buns and spoon over the beef cheek mix, then sprinkle with cheese.

MEXICAN DOG (CHIHUAHUA)

PICO DE GALLO
3 large tomatoes, deseeded and diced
½ red onion, diced
1 jalapeño, deseeded and diced
1 clove garlic, diced
½ cucumber, deseeded and diced
juice of 2 limes
¼ cup coriander/cilantro leaves, chopped
1 teaspoon Tabasco
salt and pepper, to taste

6 hot dog buns
6 hot dog frankfurters
1 cup grated mature sharp cheddar cheese
1 cup crushed corn chips

To make the Pico de Gallo, combine all the ingredients in a bowl and set aside.

Cut the hot dog buns vertically down the middle and set aside. Cook the hot dogs according to packet instructions; you can either place them in boiling water, or on a griddle pan or frying pan.

Place the frankfurters inside the buns and spoon over the Pico de Gallo. Sprinkle with cheese and crushed corn chips.

SERVES 6

THE MAX DOG (BLTD)

150 g/5 oz smoky bacon, diced
1 red chilli, diced
3 cloves garlic, minced
1 brown onion, diced
3 tomatoes, deseeded and diced
6 hot dog buns
6 hot dog frankfurters
200 g/7 oz iceberg lettuce, shredded
4 spring onions/scallions, chopped

Place the bacon, chilli, garlic and onion in a cold pan and bring the heat up to medium and sauté for 5 minutes. Turn off the heat and toss the tomatoes through the bacon and onion mix.

Cut the hot dog buns vertically down the middle and set aside. Cook the hot dogs according to packet instructions; you can either cook them in boiling water, or on a griddle pan or frying pan.

Place the frankfurters inside the buns. Add a handful of lettuce and spoon the tomato and bacon mix over the top and sprinkle with some chopped spring onions.

THE MOLLIE DOG (FRANK AND BEANS)

6 hot dog buns
6 hot dog frankfurters
6 cups Refried Beans (see recipe page 166)
100 g/3½ oz alfalfa
Pickled Jalapeño Dressing (see recipe
  page 147)
American yellow mustard

Cut the hot dog buns vertically down the middle and set aside. Cook the hot dogs according to packet instructions; you can either cook them in boiling water, or on a griddle pan or frying pan.

Spread a bun open and spoon in around 1 cup of the refried beans. Place the hot dog frankfurter on top of the beans, pipe on some mustard, add some pickled jalapeños then top with alfalfa sprouts.

SEAFOOD

CEVICHE

200 g/7 oz fresh firm fish (blue eye, king fish,
    ocean trout, tuna)
avocado mousse, to serve (see Raw Kingfish,
    Avocado Mousse, Coriander Cress,
    Jalapeño recipe page 92)
corn chips, to serve

CURING LIQUID
35 g/1¼ oz palm sugar
½ green chilli
½ red onion
100 ml/3½ fl oz freshly squeezed lime juice
50 ml/1¾ fl oz fish stock
50 ml/1¾ fl oz lemon juice
1 clove garlic
2 cm/1 in knob ginger
2 coriander sprigs
2 in/5 cm celery stalk
½ cinnamon quill
1 star anise

Make the curing liquid first. Blitz all the ingredients, except the cinnamon and star anise, in a food processor. Pour the mixture into a bowl, add the cinnamon and star anise and leave for 10 minutes for the flavours to infuse. Drain the mixture through a fine sieve and collect the curing liquid.

Prepare the fish by cutting it into strips around 5 to 8 mm/¼ to ½ in thick. Pour the liquid over the fish and place in the refrigerator for 5 minutes.

When ready to serve, place some avocado mousse on each plate. Add some cured fish and serve with the corn chips on the side. Use the corn chips to scoop up the avocado and fish mixture.

This is an absolute favourite of mine, so easy to make and so easy to eat.

COCONUT SHRIMP

3 cloves garlic, crushed

2 teaspoons ground coriander seeds

juice of 2 limes

1 teaspoon salt

1 teaspoon pepper

12 raw King, Tiger or Banana shrimp/prawns,
    shelled, deveined and butterflied

½ cup desiccated coconut

½ cup chopped chives

1 cup plain/all-purpose flour

2 eggs, beaten

oil, for deep-frying

salt and pepper to season

Mix the garlic, coriander seeds and lime juice with salt and pepper and toss through the prawns and allow to marinate for 30 minutes.

Mix together the coconut and chives in a small bowl and put the beaten eggs in another. Dust each prawn in the flour, then into the beaten egg and finally into the coconut and chive mixture.

Heat the oil in a medium saucepan to 160°C/320°F. If you don't have a thermometer, test the oil is hot enough by sprinkling some flour in the oil. If the oil bubbles, then the oil is hot enough. Fry the shrimp for about a minute or until golden.

Remove from oil, drain on absorbent paper and season with salt and pepper. Serve with chipotle mayonnaise (see Lime Mayonnaise recipe for chipotle variation page 148).

CRISPY-SKINNED FISH WITH FRESH KIWI SALSA

1 teaspoon salt

1 teaspoon pepper

1 teaspoon toasted and ground coriander seeds

1 teaspoon toasted and ground cumin seeds

pinch of chilli flakes

zest of 1 lime

¼ cup olive oil

4 x 180 g/6 oz fillets of fish, skin on (salmon, ocean trout, blue eye, stripy trumpeter)

SALSA

1 small red onion, finely diced

200 g/7 oz yellow and red cherry tomatoes, roughly chopped

1 avocado, finely diced

1 kiwi fruit, peeled and chopped

1 red chilli, deseeded and diced

10 cilantro/coriander leaves

10 mint leaves

2 teaspoons fish sauce

juice of 1 lime

1 teaspoon salt flakes

2 teaspoons palm sugar

To make the salsa, combine all the ingredients, check for seasoning and set aside.

Mix the salt, pepper, coriander seeds, cumin seeds, chilli flakes, lime zest and olive oil and brush the skin of the fish with the spice mixture.

In a large pan over medium heat, add the well-oiled fish skin-side down. Cook the fish for 5 minutes. While the fish is cooking, keep brushing the flesh with the olive oil from the pan. At the end of the 5 minutes turn the fish and cook for 30 seconds on the flesh side. Place on a warm plate and allow to rest for a minute.

Serve the fish with the salsa on the side.

SERVES 4

RAW KINGFISH, AVOCADO MOUSSE, CORIANDER CRESS, JALAPEÑO

AVOCADO MOUSSE
3 ripe avocados, flesh scooped out
1 tablespoon sour cream
juice and zest of 2 limes
2 teaspoons grated palm sugar
2 teaspoons salt
20 ml/⅔ fl oz olive oil

300 g/10½ oz kingfish (or salmon) cut into
    3mm/¼ in strips across the grain
1 jalapeño, thinly sliced
coriander cress (micro coriander)
1 tablespoon toasted pumpkin seeds
    (pepitas), seasoned
good-quality olive oil, to serve

Make the avocado mousse by putting the avocado, sour cream, lime juice and zest, palm sugar and salt in a blender. Process and slowly drizzle in the olive oil, until smooth. Set aside.

Smear the avocado mousse across your serving plate, lay the kingfish strips along the avocado, scatter over some jalapeño slices, some coriander cress and some pepitas on each piece of fish and drizzle with a little olive oil.

Serve with tostadas or a corn chip crumb.

FISH CURRY

oil, for frying

2 bay leaves

4 cloves

1 cinnamon quill

4 allspice berries

4 cardamom pods

1 onion, finely diced

1 tablespoon finely chopped coriander root

1 tablespoon grated ginger

3 cloves garlic, grated

2 teaspoons ground cumin seeds

2 teaspoons coriander seeds

½ teaspoon cayenne pepper

4 tomatoes, deseeded and diced

400 ml/14 fl oz coconut milk

250 ml/9 fl oz fish stock

500 g/17½ oz firm white-fleshed fish such as pink ling or blue eye, cut into large dices

1 cup basmati rice, cooked to packet instructions (it's important to wash the rice under hot running water after you have cooked it, so it doesn't become sticky)

coriander/cilantro leaves, to garnish

lemon or lime juice, to serve

Add a tablespoon of oil to a saucepan over medium heat and fry the bay leaves, cloves, cinnamon, allspice berries and cardamom for 2 minutes. Add the onion, coriander root, ginger and garlic and cook for 5 minutes or until onion is soft then add the cumin and coriander seeds and cayenne and cook for a further 2 minutes.

Add the tomatoes and stir for a minute. Pour in the coconut milk and stock, bring to a simmer and allow to simmer for 15 minutes.

Add the fish to the curry and place a lid on the pan. Turn off the heat and let the fish sit in the liquid for 8 to 10 minutes.

Serve the curry on top of the cooked rice and garnish with coriander leaves and a squeeze of lemon or lime juice.

This is one of those dishes that moves quickly, so it's a good idea to have everything prepared before you start so you can just add it to the pan as you go.

TUNA TEQUILA SLAMMER

120 g/4 oz tuna, king fish or snapper, diced
2 limes, cut into wedges

Curing Liquid

1 lemon, juiced

1 lime, juiced

1 orange, juiced

1 green chilli, diced

2 coriander roots

1 tablespoon palm sugar (or brown sugar)

1 teaspoon salt

1 clove garlic, diced

1 eschalot, diced

1 teaspoon coriander seeds

30 ml/1 fl oz quality blanco (white) tequila

Salsa

1 cucumber, deseeded and diced finely

1 tomato, deseeded and diced finely

1 avocado, deseeded and diced finely

1 shallot/scallion, diced finely

1 tablespoon coriander/cilantro cress (micro),
  picked, to garnish

Chipotle Salt

salt flakes

1 teaspoon of chipotle seasoning

Make the curing liquid by combining the lemon, lime and orange juice, chilli, coriander roots, sugar, salt, garlic, eschalot and coriander seeds in a blender or food processor. Let the mixture sit for 15 minutes so the flavours can infuse. Strain the mixture then add the tequila and keep the liquid refrigerated until needed.

Make the salsa by combining all of the ingredients. Mix 1 tablespoon of the prepared curing liquid and the diced king fish into the salsa.

Place 1 tablespoon of the salsa and fish mix into 12 shot glasses and pour 1 to 2 teaspoons of the curing liquid on top of the mix in each glass, then top with the coriander cress.

Mix some salt flakes with the chipotle seasoning to make chipotle salt

You can serve the limes and salt on the side—just get your guests to have a little salt, a suck of lemon and then enjoy the slammer, either by drinking it straight down or eating with a spoon. Or, before filling the glasses with the fish mixture, wipe the lime wedges around the rim of the shot glasses and roll the rims in the chipotle salt.

SERVES 4

SHRIMP CEVICHE SALAD

5 baby beetroot, cleaned and trimmed

salt and pepper, to taste

olive oil, for roasting

½ cup sugar

½ cup apple cider vinegar

2 jalapeños, cut into 5 mm/¼ in rounds

12 fresh green shrimp/prawns, shelled, tail removed, deveined and butterflied

¾ cup avocado mousse (see Raw Kingfish, Avocado Mousse, Coriander Cress, Jalapeño recipe page 92)

¼ cup shaved or shredded toasted coconut

¼ cup toasted pumpkin seeds

coriander cress (micro coriander) or purple basil

CURING LIQUID

juice of 3 limes

juice of 1 grapefruit

3 coriander roots, chopped

3 teaspoons palm sugar

1 eschalot, chopped

¼ cucumber, chopped

½ green chilli, chopped

Preheat the oven to 180°C/350°F.

Place the baby beetroot in a small foil-lined roasting tray. Season with salt and pepper and drizzle with olive oil then cover the foil over the beets and place in the oven for 30 minutes. After 30 minutes, poke the beetroot with a knife—they should be soft. Take out of the oven and set aside to cool.

Make the curing liquid by placing the lime juice, grapefruit juice, coriander roots, palm sugar, eschalot, cucumber and green chilli in a pestle and mortar or small blender and bash or process until well combined. Strain the mixture and collect the curing liquid. Put the curing liquid in a bowl and place in the refrigerator until ready to use.

Combine the sugar and vinegar in a small saucepan and bring to the boil. Take off the heat and pour the liquid over the jalapeños and set aside to cool.

Lay the shrimp in a non-metallic dish and pour the curing liquid mix over the top and allow to marinate for 5 to 10 minutes.

To serve, arrange the shrimp, roasted beetroot, avocado mousse, pickled jalapeños, toasted coconut, pumpkin seeds and coriander cress in equal amounts on each serving plate however you wish. Be as creative as you want or you can just copy me.

SERVES 6

SEARED SCALLOPS WITH HAZELNUT MOLE

1 tablespoon olive oil

12 large scallops

HAZELNUT MOLE

1¾ cups raw hazelnuts

¼ cup peanut oil

5 chipotle chillies

2 guajillo chillies

3 large tomatoes

5 cloves garlic, still in their skins

1 onion, cut into sixths

salt, for seasoning

2 teaspoons sugar

1 teaspoon salt flakes

1 teaspoon ground cumin

3 cups chicken stock

1 vanilla bean

2 bay leaves

Preheat the oven to 180°C/ 350°F.

To make the hazelnut mole, toast the hazelnuts in the oven for 15 minutes then pour onto a tea towel. Allow to cool then rub the nuts in the tea towel so the skins come off. Crush ¼ cup of the nuts in a pestle and mortar to make a nut crumb. Set the crumbs aside.

Heat the peanut oil in a medium-sized pan over a medium heat and fry the remaining whole nuts for 3 minutes. Drain the oiled nuts through a sieve and reserve the oil. Pour the oil back into the pan and fry the chipotle chillies for 3 minutes then set aside. Fry the guajillo chillies for 30 seconds then set aside.

Roast the tomatoes, garlic and onion in the oven for 25 minutes. Peel the garlic and tomatoes and then throw the tomatoes, garlic, onion and the rest of the ingredients, except the vanilla and bay leaves, into a high speed blender and blitz until smooth. You may need to blend the mixture in two batches.

Heat the leftover oil from the chillies and nuts in a large saucepan and pour the pureed ingredients in. Add the vanilla and bay leaves and allow to simmer for 10 minutes to thicken. Remove from the heat.

Heat the pan to a high heat, brush the scallops generously with olive oil and season with salt. Cook in the pan for 45 seconds then turn and cook the other side for 30 seconds.

To serve, smear some hazelnut mole on a plate, place 2 scallops on top and sprinkle with the hazelnut crumb.

Use fewer chillies if you don't want the mole to be too hot.

MEAT

ACHIOTE PORK

2 teaspoons black pepper

2 teaspoons allspice berries

1 teaspoon cumin seeds

2 tablespoons salt flakes

2 tablespoons achiote seasoning

1 tablespoon fresh lime juice

1 tablespoon fresh orange juice

1 kg/2.2 lb pork belly, diamond scored
   on the skin

Preheat the oven to 210°C/410°F.

In a dry frying pan, toast the black pepper, allspice berries and cumin seeds then add the salt and achiote seasoning. Toast for about 2 minutes or until fragrant. Crush the spices in a pestle and mortar and add the lime and orange juice to form a paste.

Rub the paste into the pork, making sure you get it in all the cuts and scores. Place the pork on a roasting rack or wire rack and roast in the oven for 20 minutes. Turn down the oven to 140°C/285°F and roast for 2½ hours.

To finish off the crackling, place it under the grill about 15 cm/6 in below the element and turn it on to medium high for about 5 minutes. Keep an eye on it as it has the tendency to burn quickly.

Serve in a taco or a torta, or with the Quinoa and Wild Rice Salad (see recipe page 142).

ADOBO ALBONDIGAS WITH SMASHED POTATOES

ADOBO ALBONDIGAS

500 g/17½ oz beef mince

500 g/17½ oz pork mince

1 egg

½ cup uncooked white rice

3 cloves garlic, grated

½ bunch coriander stalks, finely chopped

1 tablespoon ground cumin seeds

1 teaspoon chipotle seasoning
   (or 2 teaspoons smoked paprika)

1 tablespoon fresh oregano (or dried if you
   can't get fresh)

½ tablespoon salt flakes

1 tablespoon black pepper

1 small brown onion, finely diced

1 carrot, grated

50 ml/1¾ fl oz olive oil

1 quanity Three-Chilli Adobo (see recipe
   page 171)

SMASHED POTATOES

8 Dutch Cream potatoes, skin on

1 tablespoon chopped rosemary

1 tablespoon chopped thyme

50 g/1¾ oz butter

salt and pepper, to taste

½ cup grated strong cheddar cheese, to serve

Preheat the oven to 180°C/350°F.

Place both lots of mince, egg, rice, garlic, coriander, cumin, chipotle, oregano, salt, pepper, onion and carrot in a large mixing bowl. Roll up your sleeves and mix it all together with your hands, scrunching the mixture between your fingers. Once it's well combined roll into balls about the size of a golf ball and set aside.

In a large frying pan, heat a tablespoon of oil over medium heat and brown the meatballs. Once they are all browned, cover them with Three-Chilli Adobo (see recipe on page 171) and simmer for 15 to 20 minutes.

Place the whole potatoes (skin on) in a saucepan of cold water and bring to the boil and simmer until potatoes can be easily pierced with a knife. Drain the potatoes and place them in a roasting tray. Lightly crush the potatoes with the back of a spoon, spread the rosemary and thyme over the potatoes, then drizzle with the rest of the olive oil and dot with the butter. Roast in the oven for 15 to 20 minutes or until crunchy on top.

Place the potatoes on the serving plates and spoon the albondigas on top. Sprinkle with some grated cheese to serve.

Albondigas are Mexican meatballs and who doesn't love meatballs.

CHIPOTLE-BRAISED BEEF CHEEK WITH OVEN-ROASTED TOMATOES AND SMASHED POTATOES

2 chipotle chillies

2 ancho chillies

2 guajillo chillies

1 x 400 g/14 oz can tomatoes

4 beef cheeks

salt and pepper

25 ml/¾ fl oz olive oil

2 cloves garlic, minced

2 eschalots, diced

2 teaspoons ground coriander seeds

2 teaspoons ground cumin seeds

150 ml/5 fl oz red wine

15 ml/½ fl oz red wine vinegar

250 ml/9 fl oz beef stock

15 g/½ oz palm sugar, chopped

2 teaspoons dried oregano

250 ml/9 fl oz water

juice of 1 orange

8 Désirée potatoes, skin on

25 g/¾ oz butter

15 ml/½ fl oz olive oil

salt and pepper

12 truss tomatoes

To make some braising stock, toast the chillies in a dry pan for a couple of minutes each side then soak them all in water for 30 minutes. Once the chillies have softened, place them in a blender with the tomatoes and a pinch of salt. Blitz to make a puree.

Season the cheeks with salt, pepper and olive oil. Brown in a hot pan and set aside. In the same pan, sauté the garlic and eschalots in a teaspoon of olive oil for 2 minutes. Add the coriander and cumin seeds and sauté for 1 minute to release the flavour. Add the red wine and the red wine vinegar and reduce the sauce by half. Then add the tomato and chilli puree.

Return the cheeks to the pan and cover with the beef stock, adding the palm sugar and oregano. Check for seasoning and allow to simmer, covered, on the stove top or in an oven set at 150°C/300°F for 3 hours. If the sauce looks like it is drying out, add some water to thin it. Continue to add more water if you need it. Take off the lid and simmer for another 30 minutes or until the cheeks are tender and the sauce has reduced. Just before serving, add the orange juice—this will give the sauce a bit of a lift.

Recipe continued...

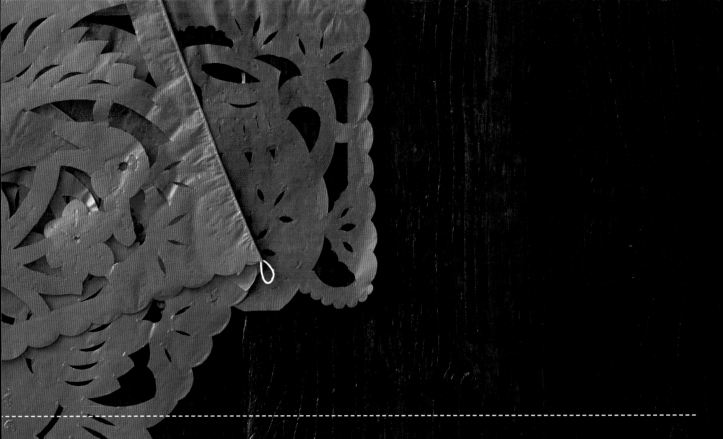

Preheat the oven to 180°C/350°F.

For the smashed potatoes, place the potatoes in a saucepan of cold water and bring to the boil. Simmer until the potatoes can be easily pierced with a knife. Drain and place in a roasting tray, crushing the potatoes with the back of a spoon or your thumb. Drizzle with olive oil and dot the butter around the pan and season with salt and pepper. Roast the potatoes for 20 minutes in the oven.

To prepare the tomatoes, place them on a roasting tray, leaving them on the vine. Season the tomatoes with salt and pepper and drizzle with olive oil. Roast at the same temperature as the potatoes for 25 minutes.

To serve, place a beef cheek on a plate and spoon over some sauce. Place some potatoes on the side and top with 2 or 3 tomatoes.

PORK CARNITAS

2 dried bay leaves

2 teaspoons dried thyme

1 teaspoon salt flakes

1 teaspoon dried marjoram

2 teaspoons achiote seasoning or paprika

1.5 kg/3 lb 5 oz pork shoulder, diced

8 cloves garlic, bruised

zest and juice of 2 oranges

1 onion, diced

3 cups water

1 tablespoon sweetened condensed milk

80 ml/2½ fl oz vegetable oil

In a pestle and mortar, crush the bay leaves, thyme, salt, marjoram and achiote them massage the mixture into the pork and allow to marinate for 2 hours.

Preheat the oven to 200°C/400°F.

Once the meat is ready, place the pork and all the remaining ingredients, except the vegetable oil, in an ovenproof saucepan or casserole dish and bring the mixture to a simmer. Allow to simmer for 1½ hours until the pork is tender. Remove the pork and reduce the sauce until it is thick and sticky. Replace the pork, pour in the oil and stir.

Place the mixture in the oven and roast for 20 minutes or until the edges are crispy.

Once the pork is crispy remove it from the oven and serve it however you like. You can shred the meat and use it as a filling for tacos, burritos, tortas or anyway you like to serve slow-cooked pork.

This is one of my favourite dishes. It can be served on its own as antojitos or in tacos with any salsa or refried beans.

CHICKEN FAJITAS

MARINADE
juice and zest of 3 limes
30 g/1 oz palm sugar
2 cloves garlic, sliced
2 teaspoons dried oregano
2 teaspoons dried thyme
1 teaspoon cayenne pepper
1 teaspoon cumin
1 teaspoon cinnamon
salt and pepper
1 tablespoon olive oil

3 chicken breasts, cut into strips or 6 chicken
    thigh fillets, cut into strips

2 tablespoons olive oil
2 onions, cut in half and sliced
1 small green capsicum/bell pepper, cut
    into strips
1 small red capsicum/bell pepper, cut
    into strips
1 small yellow capsicum/bell pepper, cut
    into strips
8 Homemade Flour Tortillas (see recipe
    page 27)
Guacamole (see recipe page 169)
Pico de Gallo salsa (see Mexican Dog recipe
    page 84)

To make the marinade, mix together the lime juice and zest, sugar, garlic, oregano, thyme, cayenne, cumin, cinnamon, salt, pepper and 1 tablespoon of olive oil. Coat the chicken pieces in the marinade and leave in the refrigerator for 30 minutes.

Heat the rest of the oil in a large frying pan over a high heat. Sauté the marinated chicken for 5 minutes. Add the onion and peppers and cook for another 5 minutes or until the chicken is cooked through.

Warm the tortillas in a dry frying pan. Spoon some of the chicken mixture down the middle of each tortilla, then spoon on some guacamole and salsa. Roll the tortillas up like a cigar so they are long, thin rolls and enjoy.

SLOW-BRAISED LAMB OR GOAT

¼ cup achiote powder

1 tablespoon plain/all-purpose flour

1 teaspoon black pepper

1 teaspoon ground cumin

1 tablespoon salt flakes

1 goat or lamb shoulder, cut into large chunks

1 tablespoon olive oil

2 brown onions, peeled and finely chopped

8 cloves garlic, crushed

2 x 400 g/14 oz cans diced tomatoes

2 cups chicken stock

3 tablespoons apple cider vinegar

6 Désirée potatoes, quartered

1 tablespoon dried oregano

1 lime, cut into wedges, to serve

½ cup coriander/cilantro, chopped, for garnish

Mexican Red Rice (see recipe page 158), to serve

Combine the achiote powder, flour, black pepper, cumin and salt and roll the shoulder chunks in the mixture. Heat the olive oil in a large frying pan, brown the shoulder chunks and set aside.

Add the onion and garlic to the same pan and sauté for 10 minutes—you may need to add a little more oil. Return the shoulder chunks to the pan and add the tomatoes, stock and vinegar and bring to the simmer. Check for seasoning then put a lid on the pan and allow to simmer for 2½ hours, checking every 30 minutes.

Take the lid off the pan and add the potatoes and oregano. Allow to simmer for another 20 minutes as the sauce reduces. It is cooked once the potatoes are tender.

Serve garnished with a wedge of lime and freshly chopped coriander with a side of red rice.

MY MEXICAN PHO

5 cherry tomatoes
3 cm/1 in knob ginger, chopped
5 cloves garlic
3 coriander roots, finely chopped
1 small red onion, roughly chopped
1 stalk of lemongrass, chopped
3 red chillies, chopped
1 tablespoon peanut oil
1 chicken breast, thinly sliced
1 chorizo sausage, roughly diced
1 L/36 fl oz chicken stock
2 teaspoons palm sugar
1 teaspoon salt flakes

juice of 1 lime
50 g/1¾ oz vermicelli noodles
picked coriander/cilantro leaves, to garnish

Place the tomatoes, ginger, garlic, coriander, onion, lemongrass and chilli in a pestle and mortar or blender and roughly pound or blitz.

Heat the oil in a hot wok until it shimmers then place the tomato-chilli mixture and fry for 2 minutes until fragrant. Add the chicken and chorizo and fry for another 5 minutes until brown.

Add the chicken stock and bring to the boil, then add the palm sugar, salt and lime juice. Check for seasoning and 3 minutes before you are about to serve add the uncooked noodles. Once they have softened, serve the soup garnished with fresh coriander.

There's a bit of Asian inspiration in this one. Asian cuisine has borrowed so much from Mexican that I think it would be OK every now and then to bring a little inspiration back.

MY TOTOPOS SOUP

350 g/12 oz secondary cut beef (chuck or
   gravy), diced
salt flakes and pepper
1 tablespoon olive oil
2 onions, finely diced
2 cloves garlic, minced
2 green chillies, finely diced
30 ml/1 fl oz tomato paste
1 teaspoon ground cumin seeds
1 x 400 g/14 oz can refried beans
3 tomatoes, deseeded and diced
1 L/36 fl oz beef stock
2 bay leaves

1 x 400 g/14 oz can beans—kidney, pinto or
   similar
100 g/3½ oz tortilla chips or Homemade
   Tostadas (see recipe page 28)
200 g/7 oz sharp cheddar cheese, grated
½ bunch coriander/cilantro leaves, chopped

Season the meat with salt flakes and pepper. Heat the oil in a large saucepan until hot and brown the meat. Once browned, remove the meat from the pan and set aside. Turn down the heat to medium and sauté the onion, garlic and chillies for 10 minutes. Add the tomato paste and cumin and cook for 1 minute.

Add the refried beans and tomatoes to the pot and stir to combine. Add the stock and the bay leaves and allow to simmer for 2 hours with a lid on.

Take the lid off the pot and add the other beans and simmer for 5 minutes.

Ladle the soup into a bowl then top with corn chips (topos), cheese and fresh coriander.

SERVES 4

MEXICAN JERK CHICKEN

8 chicken pieces
¼ cup olive oil, for basting

MARINADE
1 teaspoon allspice
1 teaspoon ground coriander seeds
1 teaspoon dried thyme
1 teaspoon cinnamon
1 teaspoon salt flakes
1 teaspoon cracked black pepper
pinch of nutmeg
15 g/½ oz palm sugar
3 cloves garlic, diced

¼ white onion, diced
3 spring onions/scallions, chopped
1 tablespoon white wine
1 tablespoon lime juice
1 red chilli, diced
15 g/½ oz palm sugar
1 tablespoon olive oil

Combine all the ingredients for the marinade and mix well.

Score the chicken pieces and rub in the marinade, place in a non-metallic dish and let sit in the refrigerator for 6 hours.

Take the chicken out of the refrigerator and allow to come to room temperature. Heat a griddle pan or barbecue to a medium heat, brush the chicken with oil and shake off any excess marinade. Fry the chicken pieces, turning regularly for 30 minutes or until the juices run clear when pierced with a knife.

Serve this with Mexican Red Rice (see recipe page 158).

MEXICAN FRIED CHICKEN

1 teaspoon chipotle seasoning (or smoked
  paprika)
1 teaspoon garlic powder
1 teaspoon crushed black pepper
1 teaspoon salt flakes
1 teaspoon paprika
4 chicken drumsticks
4 chicken thighs
1 cup milk

50 g/1¾ oz plain/all-purpose flour
oil, for frying

Preheat the oven to 180°C/350°F.

Mix together the chipotle seasoning, garlic powder, black pepper, salt and paprika. Rub the seasoning into the chicken pieces and allow to marinate for at least 2 hours.

Pour the milk over the chicken then dust in the flour.

Heat the oil in a frying pan over a high heat and fry the chicken one piece at a time to brown the coating. Place on a baking paper-lined oven tray. Once all the chicken has been fried, place in the oven for 15 minutes to finish off the cooking process.

Serve however you like.

OAXACAN BLACK MOLE

5 guajillo chillies

5 ancho chillies

5 mulato chillies

5 pasilla chillies

2 corn tortillas

3 tomatoes

5 tomatillos

¾ cups canola oil

1 ripe banana, cut in slices

2 cm/1 in knob of ginger

1 small French baguette or sourdough bread roll

4 bay leaves

¼ cup raw peanuts

¼ cup raw almonds

¼ cup raw pecans

¼ cup raisins

¼ cup sesame seeds

1 stick cinnamon

10 whole black peppercorns

4 allspice berries

4 cloves

1 white onion, cut into rounds

6 cloves garlic, diced

3 cups water

1 teaspoon dried oregano

1 teaspoon dried marjoram

1 tablespoon sugar

120 g/4 oz dark bitter chocolate, broken into chunks

4 chicken maryland (legs of thigh and drumstick) (about 1 kg/36 oz)

Preheat the oven to 180°C/350°F.

Toast all the chillies together in a large saucepan, then soak them in a bowl of water for 30 minutes.

Toast the tortillas in a pan until blackened. Set aside

Score the tomatoes and tomatillos. Place them on a roasting tray and roast in the oven for 30 minutes. Remove from the oven, allow to cool then peel off the skin and scrape the seeds out.

In a medium pan, heat the oil and fry the following ingredients separately then scoop out with a slotted spoon and place everything together in a large mixing bowl.

Fry the banana, until it browns on each side, about 5 minutes. Fry the ginger, until browned on both sides, about 2 minutes. Fry the baguette, turning until browned, about 2 minutes. Fry the bay leaves until brown, about 1 minute. Fry the peanuts, stirring until golden, about 2 minutes. Fry the almonds, stirring until golden,

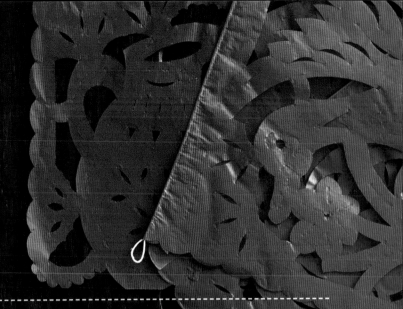

about 2 minutes. Fry the pecans, stirring until golden, about 2 minutes. Fry the raisins, stirring until puffed, about 30 seconds.

Fry the sesame seeds, along with the cinnamon stick, peppercorns, allspice and cloves until golden, about 1 minute. Drain this last batch through a sieve, reserving the oil, and add it to the bowl with the rest of the ingredients.

Sauté the onion and garlic in a pan with a little oil over a medium heat until brown, about 15 minutes, and set aside.

Drain the chillies that have been soaking and devein and deseed them. Place in a blender with the 3 cups of water and blend until smooth (this may need to be done in two batches). Set aside.

Combine the tomato and tomatillo mix with the fried spices mixture, including the onion and garlic, and blitz everything in the blender—you may need to do this in two batches.

In the frying pan, with some of the reserved oil from frying, cook the blended chilli mixture for 5 minutes then add the rest of the blended ingredients and cook down for 5 minutes. Add the oregano, marjoram, sugar and chocolate and stir until smooth—you may need to add a little more water.

Add the chicken to the mole, reduce the heat and allow to cook through, about 20 minutes.

Serve with Mexican Red or White Rice (see recipes).

This mole can be used with all white meats, but I am using chicken here. It can also be used as a filling for enchiladas. The complexity of this sauce is insane—it is a Mexican icon and one of the reasons I fell in love with the cuisine.

SALADS AND DRESSINGS

AVOCADO AND GRAPEFRUIT SALAD

¼ cup hazelnut oil

2 tablespoons white wine vinegar

salt and pepper

2 large avocados, cut into slices

1 pink grapefruit, cut into segments

1 cos lettuce

60 g/2 oz Persian feta, crumbled

- -

Whisk together the hazelnut oil and white wine vinegar with a pinch of salt and pepper.

Gently toss the avocado slices, grapefruit segments and cos lettuce together, dress with the hazelnut vinaigrette and crumble the feta over the top.

AVOCADO DRESSING

½ cup grapeseed oil

¼ cup freshly squeezed lime juice

1 clove garlic

½ cup mayonnaise (kewpie is best)

1 tablespoon Worcestershire sauce

½ ripe avocado

½ cup chopped coriander/cilantro leaves

3 tablespoons cold water

salt and pepper, to taste

Place all the ingredients into a blender and blitz until smooth.

Serve as a side to any tortilla or tostada dish or as a topping.

AVOCADO, PERSIAN FETA AND BACON SALAD

4 slices streaky bacon

2 avocados

¼ cup freshly squeezed lime juice

2 large handfuls baby butterleaf or cos lettuce

¼ cup pepitas/pumpkin seeds, toasted

60 g/2 oz Persian feta, broken into chunks

VINAIGRETTE

¼ cup olive oil

1 tablespoon honey

pinch of salt and pepper

Place the bacon in a cold pan and bring up to a medium heat. Cook until the bacon is crispy, then set aside.

Cut the avocados into strips and drizzle with a tablespoon of the lime juice and set aside

Make a vinaigrette, by combining the oil, honey, a pinch of salt and pepper and remaining lime juice and whisk to emulsify.

In a bowl, place the lettuce, avocados, bacon and scatter over the pepitas and feta. Dress the salad with the vinaigrette.

CHORIZO DRESSING

2 chorizo sausages
½ cup light olive oil
2 cloves garlic, sliced
1 teaspoon dried oregano
1 teaspoon smoked paprika
1 tablespoon fresh oregano
¼ cup fresh lemon juice
zest of 1 lime
salt flakes, to taste

Peel the chorizo and discard the skin, then cut the meat into a fine dice and place in a cold pan. Add the olive oil, garlic, dried oregano and paprika and cook on a low to medium heat until all the flavour has been extracted. This should take about 10 minutes.

Strain the oil from the sausages and set the oil and the meat aside in separate bowls.

Add the fresh oregano to the oil. Just before serving, whisk in the lemon juice, lime zest and salt flakes, to taste.

The chorizo and garlic isn't used in the dressing, but the mixture will make a fantastic crumb topping to the Avocado, Persian Feta and Bacon Salad (see recipe page 137). Or try it as a spicy alternative to oysters Kilpatrick.

This dressing is super easy but will lift any meal. It's great drizzled over the top of refried beans.

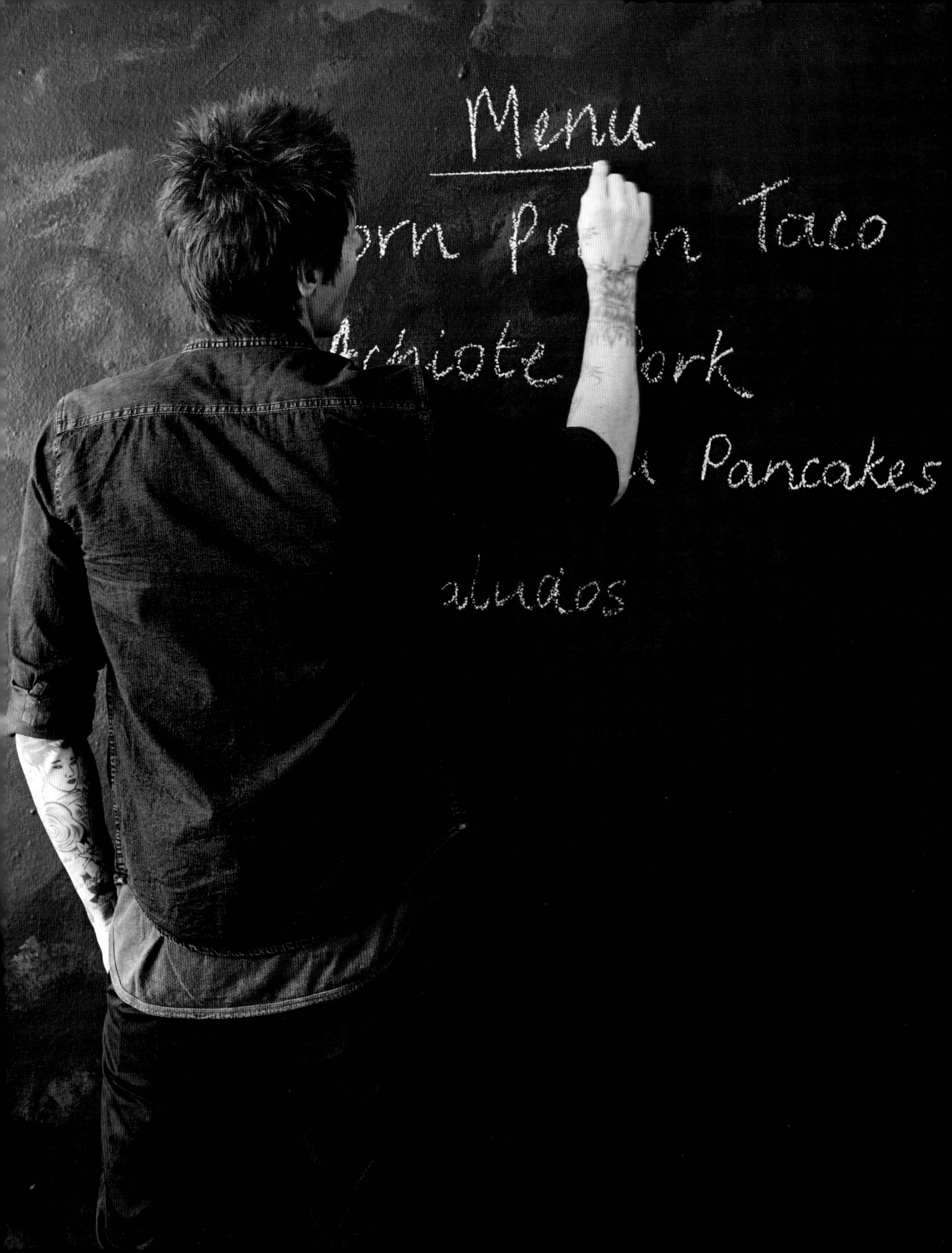
Menu
Taco
Pancakes

QUINOA AND WILD RICE SALAD

1 cup quinoa

1 cup wild rice

½ cucumber, deseeded and roughly chopped

1 tomato, deseeded and roughly chopped

4 scallions/spring onions, sliced diagonally

¼ cup chopped mint

¼ cup chopped flat-leaf parsley

¼ cup chopped coriander/cilantro leaves

CITRUS VINAIGRETTE

juice of 2 limes

juice of 1 orange

¼ cup olive oil

2 green chillies, deseeded and diced

2 cloves garlic, diced

salt and pepper

Wash the quinoa and wild rice by placing them in two separate sieves and running cold water over them. Using two saucepans, place the quinoa in one saucepan and wild rice in another. Cover them both with cold water. Bring the quinoa to the boil and allow to simmer for 12 minutes or until cooked. Strain and allow to cool. Bring the wild rice to the boil and allow to simmer for 45 minutes or until cooked. Strain and allow to cool.

Make the citrus vinaigrette by whisking together the lime and orange juice and oil, then add the chillies and garlic and season with salt and pepper.

Toss the cucumber, tomato, scallion, cold quinoa and wild rice and fresh herbs together and dress with the citrus vinaigrette.

LIME CORIANDER DRESSING

½ cup grapeseed oil

1 teaspoon grated lime zest

¼ cup fresh lime juice

¼ cup finely chopped coriander/cilantro stalk

1 teaspoon toasted and coarsely crushed
    coriander seeds

½ teaspoon grated palm sugar

salt and pepper, to taste

Combine all the ingredients in a jar and shake, then spoon or drizzle over your favourite salad or even fish or chicken.

PICKLED JALAPEÑO DRESSING

3 jalapeños
¼ cup caster/superfine sugar
¼ cup apple cider vinegar
¾ cup grapeseed oil
1 teaspoon salt
1 teaspoon pepper

- -

Deseed the jalapeños, if you don't like them too hot, and then dice.

Heat sugar and vinegar in a small saucepan until the sugar has dissolved. Allow the vinegar to cool a little then pour it over the diced jalapeños.

Let the mixture stand for 5 minutes for the flavour to infuse then put all the ingredients in a jar and shake and you're ready to go.

LIME MAYONNAISE

4 egg yolks
zest of 1 lime
30 ml/1 fl oz lime juice
10 g/1/3 oz Dijon mustard
500 ml/17½ fl oz vegetable oil
salt and pepper

Put egg yolks, zest, juice and Dijon mustard in a bowl and slowly combine with a whisk.

Once everything is well combined, slowly pour in the vegetable oil while continuously whisking to emulsify, then season with salt and pepper.

CHIPOTLE MAYONNAISE: TO MAKE CHIPOTLE MAYONNAISE, ADD A TABLESPOON OF CHIPOTLE SEASONING TO THE LIME MAYONNAISE.

SALSAS, SIDES AND SAUCES

CHIPOTLE RED SAUCE

500 g/1 lb tomatoes
1 teaspoon salt flakes
1 teaspoon black pepper
5 chipotle chillies
3 cloves garlic
150 ml/5 fl oz red wine
1 teaspoon dried oregano
¼ cup honey
1 teaspoon American yellow mustard

Preheat the oven to 180°C/350°F.

Place the tomatoes on a roasting tray, season with salt and pepper and roast for 45 minutes. Place the tomatoes in a large bowl and cover with plastic wrap and set aside for 5 minutes.

Place the dried chillies into a pan over a medium heat. As the chillies toast they will start to become more pliable, change colour a little and give off a sweet, chilli aroma. They will need only a couple of minutes each side to come to life. Once they are cooked put them in a large bowl of water and set aside for 30 minutes.

Remove the plastic wrap from the bowl of roasted tomatoes and peel the skin off the tomatoes. Place them in a blender with all the other ingredients including the enlarged chillies and blitz until smooth, then pour the sauce into a saucepan and bring to a simmer and reduce the mixture by half.

This sauce can be served hot or cold, used as a dipping sauce or poured over enchiladas or tacos.

GARLIC-LIME-CHILLI MARINADE

6 cloves garlic

1 tablespoon chipotle seasoning or
   chilli powder

60 ml/2 fl oz olive oil

125 ml/4 fl oz fresh squeezed lime juice

1 teaspoon salt flakes

Place all ingredients in a pestle and mortar or hand blender and process.

Brush the marinade over chicken, pork or fish and allow it to marinate for at least 2 hours.

Store it in an air-tight container in the refrigerator. It should keep for about a week.

FRIJOLES

100 g/3½ oz smoked bacon, finely diced
3 cloves garlic
1 onion, diced
2 x 400 g/14 oz cans pinto beans
120 ml/4 fl oz clean, crisp beer
2 tomatoes, deseeded and diced
½ cup pickled jalapeños
50 g/1¾ oz brown sugar

Put the bacon, garlic and onion in a cold saucepan and bring up to a medium heat. Cook some fat out of the bacon and cook the onion and garlic for about 5 minutes or until they soften.

Add the drained pinto beans to the pan with the beer and cook until the beer evaporates by half. Add the tomatoes and jalapeños. Cook for another 5 minutes then add the brown sugar and cook until the sugar has dissolved.

Serve as a filling in empanadas or tacos, or as a side for most meat dishes.

SERVES 4-6

MEXICAN RATATOUILLE

1 white onion, finely chopped

1 green chilli, diced

2 cloves garlic

¼ cup olive oil

2 cups fresh corn kernels

2 teaspoons fresh oregano

½ teaspoon ground nutmeg

500 g/1 lb zucchini/courgette, diced

500 g/1 lb tomatoes, deseeded and diced

½ cup cream

1 cup grated sharp cheddar cheese

salt, to taste

pepper, to taste

1 cup chopped coriander/cilantro leaves

In a large frying pan, sauté the onion, chilli, garlic in the oil for 3 minutes. Add the corn, oregano and nutmeg and sauté for another 5 to 10 minutes or until the corn starts to brown.

Add the zucchini and cook until the zucchini starts to soften, then add the tomatoes, cream, cheese and seasoning to taste. Allow the cheese to melt and turn off the heat.

Stir in the coriander just before serving.

This is a delicious and healthy side to serve with chicken or fish or just serve it stirred through some cooked pasta.

SERVES 4-6

MEXICAN RED RICE

2 cups basmati rice
500 g/17½ oz tomatoes, deseeded and
   roughly chopped
1 white onion, diced
2 cloves garlic
1 clove
1 allspice berry
1 bay leaf
1 cup water

1 teaspoon salt flakes
¼ cup grapeseed oil

- -

Rinse the rice thoroughly under cold running water until the water runs clear—this can take up to 10 minutes.

Place the tomatoes, onion, garlic, clove, allspice, bay leaf, water and salt in a blender and process until smooth. Add enough water to get 4½ cups of tomato mixture. Set aside for 15 minutes, before straining through a large mesh sieve into a large bowl.

Heat the oil in a large frying pan then add the rice and fry for about 10 minutes until it starts to become translucent. Add the tomato mixture to the rice and bring to the boil. Cook, uncovered, for 5 minutes or until the top of the rice becomes visible. Cover the pot and cook gently on a low heat for another 10 minutes. Turn the heat off and allow the rice to stand for 10 minutes.

MEXICAN WHITE RICE

2 cups basmati rice
1 white onion, diced
2 cloves garlic
1 jalapeño chilli
4 cups water
1 teaspoon salt flakes
¼ cup grapeseed oil
½ cup parsley, chopped

- -

Rinse the rice thoroughly under cold running water until the water runs clear, this can take up to 10 minutes.

Place the onion, garlic, chilli, water and salt in a blender and process until smooth.

Heat the oil in a large frying pan then add the rice. Fry the rice for about 10 minutes until it starts to become translucent, add the water and chilli mixture to the rice and bring to the boil. Cook, uncovered, for 5 minutes or until the top of the rice becomes visible. Cover the pot and cook gently on a low heat for another 10 minutes. Turn the heat off and allow the rice to stand for 10 minutes. Stir through the parsley.

MY JAFFA MOLE

1 tablespoon olive oil
1 kg/36 oz gravy beef, cut into chunks
1 brown onion, diced
3 cloves garlic, crushed
2 teaspoons ground cumin seeds
1 teaspoon cayenne pepper
200 ml/7 fl oz red wine
2 x 400 g/14 oz cans diced tomatoes
250 ml/9 fl oz beef stock

juice of 1 orange
zest of 2 oranges
3 teaspoons red wine vinegar
3 teaspoons palm sugar, chopped
70 g/2½ oz dark bitter chocolate
5 guajilla chillies
5 ancho chillies

Heat the olive oil and brown the beef in a large saucepan. Remove the beef and set aside. Add the onion and garlic to the same pan and sauté for 5 minutes. Add the cumin and cayenne and return the beef to the pan and pour in the red wine; reduce the sauce by half.

Add the remaining ingredients to the saucepan, tasting and checking for balance—add the chillies whole and you can take them out at the end of the braising time.

Allow the meat to braise for 3 hours on a low heat or until the beef is tender.

Serve with smashed or mashed potatoes or Mexican red rice.

RED SAUCE

200 g/7 oz tomatoes, deseeded and
  quartered

2 capsicums/bell peppers, deseeded and
  quartered

3 cloves garlic, in their skins

salt and pepper, to taste

2 ancho chillies

2 guajillo chillies

2 tablespoons tomato paste

1 teaspoon dried oregano

1 teaspoon brown sugar

1 cup chicken stock

- -

Preheat the oven to 180°C/350°F.

Place the tomatoes, capsicums and garlic on a roasting tray and season with salt and pepper. Roast everything for 45 minutes then place it all in a large bowl and cover with plastic wrap and set aside for 5 minutes.

Place the dried chillies into a saucepan and turn the heat up to medium. As the chillies toast they will start to become more pliable, change colour a little and give off a sweet, chilli aroma. They will need only a couple of minutes each side to come to life. Once they are ready put them in a large bowl of water and set aside for 30 minutes.

Uncover the roasted vegetables and peel the skin off the tomatoes and garlic and place everything in a blender.

Add the softened chillies to the blender with all the other ingredients and blitz until smooth. Pour the mixture into a saucepan and bring to a simmer and reduce by half

This sauce can be used as a dipping sauce or poured over enchiladas or tacos.

REFRIED BEANS

2 tablespoons olive oil

2 onions, finely chopped

2 cloves garlic, minced

1 teaspoon ground cumin seeds

1 teaspoon ground coriander seeds

1 quantity Frijoles (see recipe page 155)

50 g/1¾ oz Persian feta

¼ cup fresh chopped coriander/cilantro

In a medium-sized saucepan, add the oil, onion, garlic, cumin and coriander seeds and cook over a low heat for about 20 minutes or until the onions are soft and have caramelised a little.

Add the frijoles to the pan and fry until the beans can be mashed.

Crumble the feta over the top of the beans and dress with the chopped fresh coriander.

ROASTED SPICED PUMPKIN

1 kg/36 oz pumpkin, skin on
75 g/2½ oz butter, melted
2 teaspoons Tabasco
1 teaspoon salt flakes
1 teaspoon allspice
1 teaspoon cinnamon
¼ cup chopped parsley
¼ cup chopped coriander/cilantro
½ cup grated pecorino

½ cup crème fraîche
salsa (your choice), to serve

Preheat oven to 210°C/410°F. Line 2 large baking trays with aluminium foil.

Cut the pumpkin into wedges, leaving the skin on, and scoop out the seeds. Place the pumpkin on the baking trays. Mix the melted butter and Tabasco together and drizzle over the pumpkin.

Mix together the salt, allspice and cinnamon and sprinkle over the pumpkin.

Roast the pumpkin for 25 minutes or until tender. Take out of the oven and place in a large bowl with the herbs and pecorino.

Serve with crème fraîche and salsa of your choice.

GUACAMOLE

2 avocados, diced
1 tablespoon diced green chilli
juice of 1 lime
1 teaspoon salt flakes
¼ red onion, finely diced
2 tablespoons chopped coriander/cilantro
    leaves
1 large tomato, deseeded and diced

To make guacamole, place the avocados in a bowl and roughly mash. Add in the chilli, lime juice, salt and onion and stir to combine.

Just before serving, mix in the coriander leaves and diced tomato. Serve with corn chips or use as a filling for tacos or quesadillas.

SERVES 4-6

THREE-CHILLI ADOBO

3 guajillo chillies

3 ancho chillies

3 pasilla chillies

2 x 400 g/14 oz crushed tomatoes

8 cloves garlic

1 teaspoon salt flakes

1 teaspoon cumin seeds

1 stick cinnamon

3 cloves

8 allspice berries

Toast the guajillo, ancho and pasilla chilies in a dry pan for a couple of minutes each side then soak in a bowl of water for 30 minutes. Once the chillies have softened, place them in a blender with 1 can of tomatoes, garlic and salt and blitz to make a puree.

Pour the puree into a pan and add the other can of tomatoes, cumin seeds, cinnamon, cloves and allspice and bring to the boil. Boil for about 5 minutes.

This adobo can be used to braise meats or as a sauce or a salsa on its own with corn chips.

SALSA VERDE

500 g/17½ oz tomatillos

6 coriander/cilantro stalks

2 cloves garlic

¼ white onion, roughly chopped

2 green chillies, roughly chopped (if you don't like heat, scrape out the seeds)

1 tablespoon freshly squeezed lime juice

1 teaspoon salt

1 ripe avocado, chopped

1 teaspoon chipotle seasoning

10 g/¹⁄₃ oz palm sugar

corn chips, to serve

Place everything in a blender and blitz until smooth. Check for seasoning and pour into serving bowls with some corn chips and go nuts.

SWEETS

APPLE CRUMBLE CAKE

250 g/9 oz butter

250 g/9 oz caster/superfine sugar

4 eggs

450 g/15 oz self-raising/self-rising flour

3 large Granny Smith apples

1 teaspoon cinnamon

CRUMBLE TOPPING

¾ cup demerara sugar

1 cup plain/all-purpose flour

2 teaspoons cinnamon

1 cup desiccated coconut

115 g/3½ oz butter

1 teaspoon allspice

¼ cup chopped almonds

Preheat the oven to 180°C/350°F and grease and line a 25 cm/10 in round cake tin.

Make crumble by combining all the ingredients in a bowl and rubbing everything together with your fingertips until it resembles breadcrumbs.

To make the cake, cream the butter and sugar with electric beaters until light and fluffy. Add the eggs one at a time until well incorporated. Sift in half the flour while the beaters are still going. Fold in the rest of the flour with a spatula.

Peel and core the apples then grate them and sprinkle with the cinnamon. Spoon half the cake mixture into the tin and spread the mixture with a spatula. Cover the batter with the grated apple and then spoon over with the rest of the cake mixture. Cover the top with the crumble mixture.

Bake in the oven for 1 hour, if the top starts to brown too much cover with a little foil. Turn out and allow to cool on a wire rack.

Serve with some clotted cream and a cup of tea.

TAMALE

2 cups masa harina

1 teaspoon salt flakes

1 teaspoon baking powder

1¾ cups warm water

¾ cup sugar

75 g/2½ oz butter

a little milk

16 corn husks or banana leaves, soaked
   in water

1 cup chopped dried fruit (such as apricots,
   prunes, peach)

CRÈME PATISSIERE

350 ml/12 fl oz cream

1 teaspoon vanilla paste

¼ cup sugar

4 egg yolks

3 teaspoons cornflour/cornstarch

To make the crème patissiere, bring the cream and vanilla to a gentle simmer in a medium saucepan. Meanwhile, in a mixing bowl whisk together the sugar and egg yolks until pale and fluffy.

Slowly pour the cream into the egg mixture, continually whisking so the egg doesn't cook. Once all the mixture is incorporated pour it back into the saucepan. Slowly bring the heat up until the mixture thickens and coats the back of a wooden spoon. Sift in the corn flour and whisk the mixture together to incorporate it. Take the saucepan off the heat and allow to cool.

Combine the tamale flour, salt and baking powder with the warm water. Mix it with a wooden spoon or your hands to form a firm dough. Turn out the dough onto a floured surface and knead well for 5 minutes until it is firm and no longer tacky. Place back in the bowl and cover with plastic wrap. Allow to rest for 30 minutes.

Beat the sugar and butter until light and fluffy. Mix in half of the tamale dough and stir until incorporated. Beat in the other half of the dough (you may need to add a little milk to get the dough to come together) and continue to beat for 1 minute.

Place a steamer tray above a saucepan of boiling water. Line the steamer with 4 corn husks, then place about ½ cup of the sweetened tamale dough onto the corn husk and spread it out into a 10 cm/4 in square.

Mix 1 teaspoon of the crème patissiere with 1 tablespoon of dried fruit and place it in the middle of the tamale dough square. Pick up two sides of the corn husk and bring them together, tuck one side of the corn husk under the other. Fold the bottom of the husk and the top of the husk into the middle to make a parcel. Tie it all together with some butchers string or a strip off the corn husk (don't tie it too tight as they will expand). Lay the tamale in the steamer and repeat with the other corn husks.

Cover the steamer and steam for 1 to 1½ hours or until the filling comes away from the husks. Remove from the heat and allow to cool slightly before tucking into your tamale.

CHOCOLATE AND ESPRESSO CAKE

150 g/5 oz butter

200 g/7 oz dark chocolate

1 teaspoon vanilla paste

220 g/8 oz caster/superfine sugar

60 ml/2 fl oz espresso coffee

5 eggs, separated

120 g/4 oz self-raising/self-rising flour

TOPPING

330 ml/11 fl oz cream

1 tablespoon icing/confectioners' sugar

45 ml/1½ fl oz dark rum

250 g/9 oz punnet blueberries

Preheat the oven to 180°C/350°F. Grease and line a 24 cm/9½ in round cake tin

Combine the butter, chocolate, vanilla, sugar and espresso coffee in a saucepan over a low heat and stir until the mixture comes together smoothly. Remove from the heat and add the egg yolks, one at a time, and whisk until they have been incorporated. Add the flour and mix to combine.

Whisk the egg whites to soft peaks and then fold them gently into the chocolate mix. Pour the mix into the cake tin and bake for 55 minutes or until a skewer comes out clean, then allow to cool in the tin.

Whisk the cream, icing sugar and rum to soft peaks. Once the cake has cooled, top the cake with the whipped cream and blueberries.

SERVES 4

CHILLI STOUT CHOCOLATE POTS

Panna Cotta
3 gelatine leaves (can substitute with 3
   teaspoons of gelatin powder)
300ml/10½fl oz cream
70 g/2½ oz caster/superfine sugar
1 teaspoon cayenne pepper
150 ml/5 fl oz milk
5 cardamom pods
250 g/9 oz good-quality dark chocolate
300 ml/10½fl oz whipped cream

Vanilla Cream
300 ml/10½ fl oz cream
1 teaspoon vanilla paste
40 g/1½ oz icing/confectioner's sugar

Stout Jelly
35 g/1¼ oz caster/superfine sugar
2 teaspoons gelatine or 3 gelatine leaves
125 ml/4 fl oz hot water
375 ml/13 fl oz stout, at room temperature

Hazelnut Praline
½ cup hazelnuts
1½ cups sugar
¼ cup water

To make the panna cotta, place the gelatine leaves in cold water and set aside.

In a saucepan, mix together cream, sugar, cayenne and milk over a low heat. Squeeze the excess water from the gelatine and stir it into the heated cream until it dissolves.

On a chopping board, slightly bruise the cardamom pods with the blade of a knife in order to release their aroma, then place in the cream mixture and bring to the boil on a moderate heat. Once boiling, remove from heat and strain out the cardamom pods and return the cream mixture to the saucepan.

Break up the chocolate and add to the heated cream while still off the heat. Stir until the chocolate has melted and the mixture has a smooth consistency.

Allow mixture to cool slightly before folding in the whipped cream. Then divide equally between the pot glasses. You can use whatever size glasses you like, it will just depend on how much you want to serve your guests. Allow to set in the refrigerator (covered) for at least 4 hours.

Recipe continued...

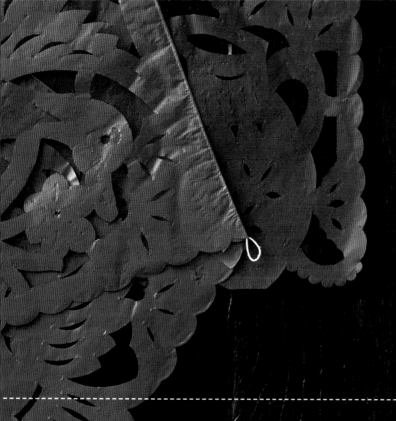

To make vanilla cream, whisk the ingredients to form soft peaks.

Make the stout jelly by dissolving the sugar and gelatine in the hot water then add the stout and allow to cool. Take the panna cottas from the refrigerator and pour enough stout mixture in each pot to cover the panna cotta with 5 to 10 mm/¼ to ½ in of jelly. Return the panna cottas to the refrigerator and allow to set.

To make the praline, spread the hazelnuts on top of a silicon mat or a baking paper-lined tray. Place the sugar and ¼ cup of water in a pan and bring to the boil. Allow to simmer until the mixture starts to turn brown, then pour the hot syrup over the hazelnuts. Set aside to cool and harden. Place chunks in a blender and blitz lightly.

Remove the pots from the refrigerator about 5 minutes before you are ready to serve. Add a layer of vanilla cream to each pot and just as you are about to serve, sprinkle them with some hazelnut praline.

BANANAS IN CARAMEL RUM

3 tablespoons dark rum

50 g/1¾ oz caster/superfine sugar

70 g/2½ oz butter

juice and zest of 1 lime

4 whole bananas, peeled

Place the rum, sugar, butter and lime juice and zest in a heavy frying pan and cook for 2 minutes until the sugar has dissolved.

Add the bananas to the pan and turn to coat. Cook the bananas over a medium heat for 5 minutes until each side is golden.

Serve with vanilla ice cream and a drizzle of the sauce from the pan

MEXICAN MESS

CARAMEL

150 g/5 oz caster/superfine sugar

1 tablespoon water

150 g/5 oz cream

50 g/1¾ oz butter

1 tablespoon salt flakes

MERINGUES

5 egg whites

80 g/2½ oz caster/superfine sugar

1 tablespoon cracked black pepper

LIME CREAM

1 teaspoon vanilla paste

1 tablespoon caster/superfine sugar

zest of 2 limes

330 ml/11 fl oz cream

Lime Sherbet (see recipe page 189)

250 g/9 oz raspberries

250 g/9 oz blackberries

First, make the caramel. Combine the sugar and water in a saucepan and simmer until it starts to turn brown and the caramel starts to form. Add the cream then the butter and stir to combine. Add the salt and set aside.

Preheat the oven to 100°C/210°F.

To make the meringues, beat the egg whites and sprinkle in the sugar as you go, until soft peaks form. Fold in the black pepper, then spoon the mixture into a piping bag.

Pipe small meringues, about the size of a 10 cent piece on to silicon paper, and bake in the oven for about 20 minutes or until they sound hollow when you flick them.

Make the lime cream, by mixing the vanilla, sugar, and lime zest into the cream and beating until soft peaks form.

To serve, assemble some crushed up meringue, some lime cream, lime sherbet, some berries in a large bowl or individual serving glasses. Add a drizzle of caramel on top.

A Mexican mess is a play on an Eton mess, so once all the components are ready the idea is that you mash them all together, to create a serendipitous dessert. Go nuts and build your own mess. You can serve this in individual bowls or as one large mess.

SERVES 8

LIME SHERBET

3 tablespoons lime jelly crystals

2 tablespoons citric acid

1 tablespoon bicarbonate of soda/baking
    soda

8 shot glasses

- -

Combine all ingredients in a mixing bowl, making sure they are well mixed. Sift them if you need to.

Spoon 2 teaspoons of the mixture into each shot glasses and have some fun.

I used to make this in my science class every year, it's a great, fun recipe. Give it a go, I promise it will make you laugh

SMASHED MOJITO CAKE

CAKE
3 egg yolks
350 g/12 oz caster/superfine sugar
150 g/5 oz butter, melted
250 ml/9 fl oz milk
1 teaspoon vanilla paste
100 g/3½ oz desiccated coconut
250 g/9 oz self-raising/self-rising flour
3 egg whites, beaten to soft peaks

MOJITO SYRUP
½ cup sugar
½ cup water
¼ cup dark rum
¼ cup lime juice
zest of 3 limes

½ bunch mint

LIME CREAM
1 teaspoon vanilla paste
1 tablespoon icing/confectioners' sugar
zest of 2 limes
330 ml/11 fl oz cream

TO SERVE
250 g/9 oz raspberries, strawberries,
   blueberries or blackberries
icing/confectioners' sugar, for dusting
picked mint leaves

Preheat the oven to 180°C/350°F. Grease and line a large-sized round cake tin.

Cream the egg yolks and sugar until pale and creamy then add the butter a little at a time until well incorporated. Add the milk, a little at a time, until everything is combined. Stir in the vanilla paste.

Fold the coconut and flour into the egg yolk mixture. When that is incorporated, gently fold in the egg whites. Pour the mixture into the cake tin and bake for 35 to 45 minutes or until a skewer comes out clean.

Make the mojito syrup by combining sugar, water and rum and bring to the boil. Simmer for 1 minute then turn off the heat and add the lime juice, zest and mint and set aside to cool, then strain.

To make the lime cream, add the vanilla, sugar and lime zest to the cream and whip until soft peaks form.

Once the cake has come out of the oven allow it to cool a little, then smash it up, smear some of the lime cream on a plate or platter add the smashed cake, some berries and mint leaves, drizzle with the mojito syrup and dust with icing sugar.

PINEAPPLE AND CHILLI UPSIDE-DOWN CAKE

125 g/4 oz butter

½ cup brown sugar

¼–½ teaspoon cayenne pepper

3 cups pineapple pieces

1½ cups self-raising/self-rising flour

½ teaspoon bicarbonate of soda/baking soda

1 teaspoon salt

¾ cup caster/superfine sugar

1 egg

¾ cup buttermilk

- -

Preheat the oven to 180°C/350°F.

In a 23 cm/9 in round ovenproof saucepan, melt the butter until it just starts to turn brown, pour the melted butter into a mixing bowl and set aside. Then sprinkle the brown sugar and cayenne pepper in the pan with the residual butter and toss in the pineapple.

In a large bowl, mix together the flour, baking soda, salt, sugar and melted butter, then add the egg and then the buttermilk until well combined.

Pour the batter over the pineapple in the pan and place the pan in the oven. Bake in the oven for 35 minutes until it is golden on top.

Remove from the oven and let cool for 10 minutes before turning it out. Serve with fresh mint and double cream.

RASPBERRY BAVAROIS

RASPBERRY COULIS
250 g/9 oz raspberries (frozen or fresh)
125 g/4 oz caster/superfine sugar
125 ml/4 fl oz water

2 egg yolks
135 g/4½ oz caster/superfine sugar
2 gelatine leaves
3 egg whites
120 ml/4 fl oz cream, whipped to
  medium peaks

Place the raspberry coulis ingredients in a small saucepan and bring the mixture to the boil. Allow to simmer for 5 minutes then strain the mixture through a fine sieve and collect the liquid. Pour the liquid back into the saucepan and bring it to a simmer. Simmer for 3 to 5 minutes then set aside to cool.

Cream the egg yolks and 35 g/1 oz sugar. In a saucepan, over a low heat, bring the coulis to just below boiling point. Add in the gelatine leaves and allow to dissolve. Pour the coulis over the egg mixture, whisking constantly so as not to split the eggs. Once everything has been combined, return the mixture to the pot and stir on a medium-high heat until the mixture thickens and covers the back of a wooden spoon.

Make an Italian meringue by melting the remaining 100 g/3½ oz sugar in a saucepan over a medium-high heat until it reaches 110°C/230°F . Whisk the egg whites and when the sugar reaches 118°C/245°F and the whites are at soft peaks slowly drizzle the sugar syrup into the egg whites while the beater is still running.

Fold together the meringue, the raspberry mix and the whipped cream and then pour the mixture into piping bags and pipe into 4 large or 8 small serving glasses, moulds or dariole moulds. Leave to set in the refrigerator for about an hour or more. Serve straight from the fridge.

MAKES ABOUT 500 G/17 OZ

CARAMELISED CHOCOLATE WALNUTS

200 g/7 oz caster/superfine sugar

80 ml/2½ fl oz water

400 g/14 oz walnut halves

2 tablespoons salt flakes

100 g/3½ oz dark chocolate, melted

- -

Preheat the oven to 160°C/320°F. Line a baking tray with baking paper/parchment.

Combine the sugar and water in a medium saucepan and bring to the boil then add the walnuts and return to the boil. Boil for 5 minutes.

Drain the walnuts through a sieve then spread them out on the lined baking tray and roast in the oven until golden, about 10 minutes (be careful as they will turn quick).

Remove the walnuts from the oven, sprinkle with the salt and allow to cool.

Once the walnuts have cooled, drizzle them with the melted choc, allow them to cool and harden before serving.

RUM AND BANANA PANCAKES

PANCAKES

2 cups self-raising/self-rising flour

1 teaspoon bicarbonate of soda

1 tablespoon caster/superfine sugar

2 eggs

50 g/1¾ oz butter, melted

1 cup milk

1 cup buttermilk

1 teaspoon vanilla paste

butter and olive oil, for frying

TOPPING

6 bananas, thickly sliced

½ cup demerara sugar

75 ml/2½ fl oz agave syrup

45 ml/1½ fl oz dark rum

1 cup Caramelised Chocolate Walnuts (see recipe page) to serve

300 ml/10½ fl oz double cream, to serve

To make the pancakes, sift the dry ingredients into a large bowl, make a well in the centre, add the eggs, butter and milk and whisk gently incorporating the dry ingredients until smooth. Add the buttermilk and vanilla and whisk again and then let the mixture rest for 30 minutes.

Heat a large frying pan over a medium heat. Melt some butter and a little olive oil and pour in ½ cup of the pancake mixture. Cook until bubbles form on top of the mixture then turn over and fry for another minute. Once browned on both sides, place the pancake on a plate and place it in the oven to keep warm. Repeat with the remaining pancake mixture, until all the mixture has been cooked.

Preheat the oven to 200°C/400°F.

Spread the bananas on a shallow roasting tray and scatter the sugar over the top. Combine the agave syrup and rum and pour over the bananas and sugar then let the bananas caramelise in the oven for 5 to 8 minutes.

Place 3 pancakes on a plate, spoon over some bananas and walnuts and dollop with a little cream.

COCONUT AND LIME PANNA COTTA WITH CANDIED HAZELNUTS

COCONUT PANNA COTTA
5 gelatine leaves (or substitute 5 teaspoons of
    gelatine powder)
420 ml/14 fl oz coconut milk
2 teaspoons vanilla paste
70 g/2 oz caster/superfine sugar

330 ml/11 fl oz cream, whipped to soft peaks

LIME SEGMENTS
½ cup caster/superfine sugar
½ cup water
3 large limes, cut into segments

CANDIED HAZELNUTS
12 toasted hazelnuts
12 toothpicks
1 cup caster/superfine sugar
¼ cup water

1 mango, cut into strips, for serving

To make the coconut panna cotta, place the gelatine in cold water and set aside.

In a medium saucepan, heat the coconut milk, vanilla and sugar over a low heat until the sugar dissolves. Squeeze the excess water from the gelatine and whisk it into the mixture. Remove from heat and allow to cool.

Slowly pour the coconut mixture into the whipped cream, folding it in as you go. Pour the mix into 4 moulds and allow to set in the refrigerator.

Meanwhile, make the lime segments. Mix together the sugar and water in a saucepan and stir, over a low heat, until the sugar dissolves. Pour the sugar syrup over the lime segments in a heatproof bowl and allow to cool.

Make the candied hazelnuts by placing the sugar and water in a saucepan and bring to the boil. Allow the mixture to simmer until it starts to turn a caramel brown and remove from heat. Stick the toothpicks into the hazelnuts. Dredge a hazelnut through the caramel and slowly raise it out of the pan and a long thread will form. Place on a lined baking tray and allow it to cool. Repeat with the remaining hazelnuts.

When you are ready to serve, remove the moulds from the refrigerator, dip the moulds into hot water then turn out onto the serving plates. Place some lime segments, 3 hazelnuts and mango strips on each plate, around the panna cotta. Alternatively, serve the panna cotta in the glass, sprinkled with lime segments, hazelnuts and mango.

SERVES 6

POLENTA CAKE WITH PINEAPPLE SYRUP

300 g/10 ½ oz caster/superfine sugar

300 g/10½ oz butter, softened

1 teaspoon vanilla paste

4 eggs

150 g/5 oz fine polenta

250 g/9 oz almond meal

50 g/1¾ oz self-raising/self-rising flour

1½ teaspoons baking powder

zest and juice of 3 limes

PINEAPPLE SYRUP

125 ml/4 fl oz pineapple juice

juice of 2 limes

50 g/1¾ oz caster/superfine sugar

double cream, to serve

Preheat the oven to 180°C/350°F.

Cream the sugar, butter and vanilla until light and fluffy. Add the eggs, one at a time, making sure each egg is incorporated before adding the next.

Fold in the polenta, almond meal, flour, baking powder and lime zest and juice. Spoon the mixture into a medium-sized, greased and lined cake tin and bake for 1 hour or until a skewer comes out clean.

To make the pineapple syrup, combine the pineapple juice, lime juice and sugar in a small saucepan and bring to a simmer then set aside.

Once the cake has come out of the oven, prick it all over with a fork and pour over the pineapple syrup. Let it soak in before serving with some double cream.

GLOSSARY

achiote: a seasoning paste made from anato seeds

adobo: a sauce or marinade used on meats

albondigas: meatballs

ancho chilli: a dried poblano chilli, fruity in flavour and a 3 on the heat
    scale

antojitos: a sudden craving or a passing whim, it is the name that is given
    to snacks in Mexico

carnitas: braised and fried pork that has been marinated in achiote

ceviche: curing of seafood with citrus fruits

chilaquiles: the closest thing you will find to nachos in Mexico

chimichangas: filled pan-fried tortilla parcels

chipotle: dried smoked jalapeños, a 7 on the heat scale

empanadas: little parcels wrapped in masa harina dough and fried

enchiladas: tortillas filled with yummy things and rolled into tubes and
    baked

fajitas: fresh flour tortillas that are filled with morsels at the table

gorditas: masa harina corn cakes, thick tostadas with heavier toppings

guajilla chilli: large dried chilli, slightly acidic and a 3 on the heat scale

habanero: a super hot little chilli, looks like a tiny capsicum a 10 on the
    heat scale

huitlacoche: referred to as corn truffles, it is actually a fungus that grows
    on corn and has an intense mushroom flavour

jalapeño: a hot green chilli, a 7 on the heat scale

Manchego cheese: a sharp crumbly cheese that melts really well
masa harina: corn flour used for making tortillas and antojitos
mole: a sauce made using nuts, seeds and fruit
molettes: a Mexican sandwich snack

Pico de Gallo: a fresh salsa made with tomatoes, chillies and white
    onion.
pinto beans: black beans used for making frioles and refried beans
poblano chillies

quesadillas: tortillas with a filling that contains cheese, they are the
    Mexican equivalent of a toasted sandwich
queso fresco: a soft white cheese similar to ricotta

sopes: small, thick tortillas made from masa harina with crimped edges,
    filled up like tarts and baked

tacos: the best known of all Mexican cuisine, the filling limited only by
    your imagination and folded in corn tortillas
tamales: cornmeal dumplings that are wrapped in corn husk and
    steamed
taquitos: mini tacos
tortas: Mexican version of a hamburger
tortillas: masa harina-based or flour-based disk or wrap
tostadas: fried tortillas, like a large corn chip
tostaditas: mini tostadas
totopos: what Westerners would call corn chips, they are fried tortilla
    triangles

ACKNOWLEDGEMENTS

I would like to acknowledge and thank all those people involved in MasterChef and New Holland Publishing for opening doors that would otherwise be locked. To my Mum, Dad, Belinda, Leigh and Grant thank you for your unconditional love and support without you all I would be lost. Finally to Sally, Max and Mollie thank you for putting up with me and inspiring me everyday.

ABOUT BEN

Ben attributes his love of food to his grandmother—she used to bake for the 40 plus tradesmen employed by the family business each morning. He remembers making scones with her after school. 'She was an amazing cook, a true grandmother. Before you said hello to her you'd be in the pantry looking at what she'd baked.'

Family is important to Ben. Growing up on the coast of Tasmania, Ben was the second of four children. 'As a child we used to go on family camping trips and we would take out Dad's boat, go fishing and cook the fish. We would go diving for abalone and cook it on the campfire. We still go diving for abalone throughout the year.'

Cooking has always been a passion for Ben. Despite first starting a career in teaching, being selected to appear on MasterChef Season 4 was a turning point for Ben and his passion for food. The experience allowed him to refine his skills, immerse himself in food and be taught by some of the most experienced chefs in the business. Since the show, opportunities to continue working with food have been widespread with Ben appearing on national morning breakfast shows and guest appearances on television cooking shows. Other major events have included celebrity cooking demonstrations at major food festivals, as well as hosting and cooking for a variety of private functions and cooking schools. He currently has an ongoing column in his local newspaper and a 'Talking Food' segment on his local radio station.

Ben's strengths are in Mexican and seafood cooking, however he is always keen to explore new, fresh ingredients and combinations of flavours. Ben's personality and down-to-earth approach have made him popular with people of all ages. His philosophy is unassuming; 'My food style is simple; take ingredients and recipes that will bring people together, combine them in a way that is interesting but achievable. Above all cook it because you love it. You have to fall in love with the process. The process of discovering the ingredients, developing the idea, creating the dish, sharing the flavour and discussing the outcome; this is what food is all about'.

INDEX

First published in 2013 by
New Holland Publishers
London • Sydney • Cape Town • Auckland
www.newhollandpublishers.com

The Chandlery Unit 114 50 Westminster Bridge Road London SE1 7QY
1/66 Gibbes Street Chatswood NSW 2067 Australia
Wembley Square First Floor Solan Road Gardens Cape Town 8001 South Africa
218 Lake Road Northcote Auckland New Zealand

A catalogue record of this book is available at the British Library and at the National Library of Australia

ISBN: 9781742574615

10 9 8 7 6 5 4 3 2 1

Managing director: Fiona Schultz
Publisher: Diane Ward
Project editor: Jodi De Vantier
Designer: Tracy Loughlin
Stylist: Bhavani Konings
Photographer: Steve Brown
Production director: Olga Dementiev
Printer: Everbest Printing Co Ltd China

A big thank-you to the following companies for the generous use of their products: Di Lorenzo Tiles, Holy Kitsch,
Market Import, Mud Australia and Paper 2.

Follow New Holland Publishers on
Facebook: www.facebook.com/NewHollandPublishers